The Gen-Z Book

The Gen-Z Book

The A to Z about Gen-Z

Riya Goel

NEW DEGREE PRESS

THE GEN-Z BOOK

The A to Z about Gen-Z

ISBN   978-1-63676-826-7   *Paperback*

978-1-63730-216-3   *Kindle Ebook*

978-1-63730-270-5   *Ebook*

To My Future Self...

and to my Nana who I wish could read this

Contents

Take a moment.

Understand the value that you hold.

— *SEEKER*

Introduction

I'm sitting down to write. I'm sixteen (as of now), and I have the world at my fingertips. That's the power of Gen-Z.

So, what is Gen-Z? It's in the title of this book. A quick search online will yield basic statistics and facts, like how Gen-Zers are born in the range of years from 1997-2012, succeeding Millennials, and preceding Generation Alpha.

Such facts define the definition. However, I'd argue that Gen-Z means so much more.

How does Gen-Z use its power? Here's a prime example.

One of my first interviews for this book was with Ava McDonald, the CEO and founder of Zfluence, an influencer marketing company. Ava got the idea for her company after scrolling on her Instagram feed. She saw a post from an influencer with a caption exactly copy-pasted from their email correspondence with the brand. How did she know? The caption for the post included every component of an email—from a greeting (ex: Dear so and so) to a thank you at the end of the email.

Ava realized that this influencer probably didn't care much about the brand, but definitely cared about the paycheck, and that's why so little thought went into the post.

This made her understand the importance of authenticity in marketing and campaigning. Her company, Zfluence, is the first and only digital solution that connects companies directly with leading members of Gen-Z who love the brands' products and want to promote them authentically to their friends and network on social media.

Now let me backtrack for a quick second. Ava formed her company in her senior year of high school (I'm a senior right now) and has already had her work featured in Forbes magazine. This sounds prodigal, and any other person could name a million excuses as to why they couldn't do the same sort of thing. But this is the nature/attitude/reality of Gen-Z. We are creators, innovators, and we're about to change the world—sooner than you might think.

Often, the kind of analysis and understanding the world has of Gen-Z is based on the views that older generations and big companies hold, because they are the ones who are impacted by new consumers in the market, and frankly, the change that Gen-Z is bringing. In general, Gen-Zers are undefined because much of our generation is still so young. The diversity and large size of our generation makes predicting anything about Gen-Z unpredictable as well.

Throughout this book, I hope to shed light on who Gen-Z is as a generation, why understanding our generation is essential, and how we're going to change the world. As a Gen-Zer myself, I bring my perspective to you, the reader, in this book to go over the good, the bad, and the everything in between for Gen-Z.

To me, Gen-Z is somewhat misunderstood, especially to other generations. If we're not misunderstood, then people simply don't understand us. Simple assumptions like "they're always on their phones," or "they're always saying some nonsense on the internet," are common one-liners I've heard when I ask people to describe Gen-Z. You might be thinking I'm going to go into a whole paragraph here explaining why such folks are incorrect, but in truth, there's validity to their claims.

Gen-Zers are on their phones. But these very devices have a plethora of uses. From SAT prep to online activism, we can do anything and everything on our devices. As far as saying anything we want on the internet, I agree that to some extent, people need to be mindful of what they put out there because everything on the internet is permanent. However, using our voices helps us create community and find people thousands of miles away from us that care about the same things that we do.

Speaking up on the internet can help us create viable social change. This could mean planning online events, protests, panels, and discussions. The internet, and being online, is our generation's defining resource that has already proved its worth during the 2020/2021 global pandemic.

So, to circle back, Gen-Z is *misunderstood, or simply not understood at all.*

Other people try to put Gen-Z in boxes, yet we are trying to break out of those very boxes to forge our own identities freely.

General blanket statements that define Gen-Z are made with negative connotations instead of viewing qualities of Gen-Z in a positive light.

Here's an update on the current state of Gen-Z

In a lot of ways, people look at Gen-Z and see a group of people who are "always on their phones," or are using social media constantly with their screen time being longer than the time they're in school. But people like Ava show us that there's immense potential to harness tools like social media and technology to be driving forces for change. When I talked to Ava, I wondered: *was her mindset unique to her, or were there some common threads within our generation that make us stand out?*

What I've found has changed the way that I see our future and the future of our generation.

Okay, so you might be thinking, who is Gen-Z? I've heard about them, but I don't really know who they are. Well, here's the run-down.

Gen-Z currently consists of seventy-two million people born in the range of years from 1997-2012, according to Pew

Research.[1] As a group, we value expression, identity, and privacy, and have a need for accountability, social good, and purpose behind the brands that we support. To my last point, we put our money where our values are—and aren't afraid to defend our opinions. We value diversity, equity, and equality, and are pretty smart. I mean, we did grow up being able to get an answer in less than a second from Google.

And yes, I understand that Google churns up all kinds of information, from Ivy League research to opinions on online forums. The information offered on Google isn't all high quality or even factual, and this poses a question; is Gen-Z more vulnerable to misinformation, propaganda, and echo chambers? Or are Gen-Zers also more skilled at sifting through the chaff? I'd say a little bit of both, but I'll go into that later.

Market research shows that 85 percent of Generation Z learns about new products on social media. They are also 59 percent more likely than older generations to connect with brands on social media too, and before making a purchase, Gen-Zers are two times more likely than Millennials to turn to YouTube.[2]

And we care, a lot. We're changing the world, and there might not be much you can do about it. This last sentence suggests Gen-Z is being opposed. In a sense, we are. Other generations, specifically older ones, doubt our abilities. The

---

1   Michael Dimock, "Defining generations: Where Millennials end and Generation Z begins, *"Pew Research Center,* January 17, 2019.

2   Dara Fontein, "Everything Social Marketers Need to Know About Generation Z," *Hootsuite,* November 13, 2019.

underlying problem, however, is that other generations are threatened by change. And this is natural, because one could argue that all generations are threatened by the ones that follow. But, Gen-Z poses an unusual amount of change in a small amount of time because every day, technology is getting more advanced. We are becoming more educated, informed, and aware.

Gen-Z feels strongly about the current political system, climate change and the future of our planet, debt and education, social media, and mental health, just to name a few. But what we're beginning to see is the emergence of intersectionality in our approach to social movements, and interconnectedness in our society and culture—which brings Gen-Z together for the most part.

Intersectionality is a concept that I'll touch upon later in the book. For now, I'll just say it brings us together because we're able to step out of our shoes and into those of others to gain new perspectives. By doing so, we're able to develop a greater sense of empathy and come together as people.

Despite the emerging power of Gen-Z, there is a misconception that we, as a group, are underwhelming. As discussed earlier, this isn't the whole story, and that is the difference between understanding versus assuming something about Gen-Z.

So, why write The Gen-Z Book?

I personally believe that Gen-Z is going to transform the world, and we have all the resources necessary to do so. We care about authenticity and aren't afraid to call people out about it. As a generation, we have a desire for social change and have access to tools like technology to use in our pursuits.

And you might think this is great! But you might be questioning why I should be writing this. Short answer? Well, I'm a Gen-Zer myself. Longer answer? I've grown up with social media my entire life, and I'm also personally curious and excited to display even a little bit of the immense potential that Gen-Z has.

This book, in a sentence, is a "Gen-Z temperature check." During the interviews that I conducted, I asked the questions: What makes Gen-Z special? What is so interesting about Gen-Z and our consumer habits that will redefine markets in the future? How will Gen-Z change the world as we know it? Gen-Z is complicated, but I'd argue *that's what makes us interesting.*

Here's a little bit about me: I'm an activist, and if we're throwing around titles, you might even consider me a micro-influencer. I've started two of my own organizations and have worked on start-ups and international boards with youth, for youth. To me, it's essential to convey and analyze what my generation will do and what is necessary in order for us to be successful and optimize our potential.

I feel as though I have a somewhat unique vantage point in this journey because I am writing about my own generation. So, the book is by youth and for the world, giving everyone an inside look at what it is like to be a part of Gen-Z and what our next steps are in the future.

But before you read the next six or so paragraphs, let me state one thing. Gen-Z is not a monolith—and to that tune, Gen-Z tends to be lumped into groups, or with Millennials; but we have our own identity, and a strong one at that.

I've talked to some of the most influential and well-regarded experts to contribute to this book, like Ziad Ahmed, the founder and CEO of JUV Consulting; Matt Sarafa, who owns and designs for his brand, Matt Sarafa; and Lucie Zhang, the director of social media at Vogue.

This book is somewhat of a summary of Gen-Z. I'm giving you the who, what, when, where, why, and how straight from leaders of my generation. If other generations don't develop a better understanding of Gen-Z, they will be left behind in our constantly shifting and changing world. If other generations don't understand us, Gen-Z won't get essential opportunities to capitalize on our vast and varying strengths.

Misunderstandings will ensue (and have already) leading to hampered communication and increased polarization in the world. This will lead to distrust, which could lead to societal schisms, intergenerational war; you get the gist. The important point is that Gen-Z is powerful. With our skillsets, abilities, and intersectional way of thinking, the world can become a better place on every front, from technology to human rights. But Gen-Z is the key to this success, and other generations need to work with us to achieve success.

Gen-Z is the Greatest "Zeneration" in my opinion, and I explore why this emerging generation is poised to right the wrongs left to us by prior generations. Gen-Z needs to be empowered to fix these wrongs because other generations either can't, or won't, deal with the issues they've left behind. But this doesn't mean that change only lies within our youngest generations.

In a few years of this book being published, Generation Alpha will be the youngest generation to date. And with technology advancing as fast as ever, the age range for each generation gets smaller. The solution lies in intergenerational unity (where generations come together over common ground), with every person, no matter where they are in life, working toward a world where the goal is betterment for society, for the world, and for all. All generations play a role in the state of the world, but currently, Gen-Zers might have a few valid ideas I believe the world should listen to.

Old and young, we all need to understand the position and opportunity that Gen-Z has in changing our world currently, and in the future. This is important because intergenerational unity is essential to moving forward in our world, and to do this, we all need to understand each other.

Parents, who are your kids going to be in the future?

CEOs and industry professionals, how are you going to make workplaces more inclusive, accessible, and adjustable to the needs of Gen-Z?

Gen-Z, how are you going to change the world?

Part I

What is change, and what is Gen-Z's role in change?

Chapter 1

The History and Science of Change

Youth are naturally poised to enact change. American psychologist Jean Twenge, the author of *iGen*, states that iGens (her name for Gen-Zers) exhibit more care for others and are respective and inclusive of diversity, leading to their involvement in social good.[3] Collectively, we want to right the wrongs of previous generations and make our lives and the lives of future generations better. But where have we seen this in history, and where does that leave us today?

According to Erin Blackmore of *National Geographic*, youth and youth activists have fueled five movements: the civil rights movement, Vietnam war protests, Tiananmen Square, Arab Spring, and Indigenous water rights. Youth have also been instrumental in other movements, such as climate change, women's marches, equal rights, racial inequality,

---

3   Diana Divecha, "How Teens Today Are Different from Past Generations," *Greater Good Magazine*, October 20, 2017.

and more.[4] The common link in all of these movements? Youth. But why? How? Where?

Let's look at these five movements more closely. According to the article by Blakemore, "Youth were instrumental in the civil rights movement's most memorable moments," pushing forward voting rights, the desegregation of schools, and advocating for legislation. "Youth who participated in the Civil Rights movement embraced what one-time SNCC chairman Representative John Lewis called 'good trouble'— fearless agitation designed to provoke, challenge, and move progress forward."[5]

In the Vietnamese war protests, "students marched, conducted sit-ins, and agitated against the war. The protests electrified and divided the American public." In Tiananmen Square, "youth demanded democratic reforms and economic liberalization in the face of cronyism and economic decline." In Arab Spring, youth took part in a wave of "pro-democracy protests." And in the fight for Indigenous water rights, youth "sparked outrage that drew thousands of demonstrators to an encampment that soon became the site of protests and arrests."[6]

Now, this is power. This means change. But it poses a question: are youth set up to be catalysts for change? Or, do youth set themselves up? The answer is simple. Youth have a desire for change. Youth don't need an invitation

---

4   Erin Blakemore, "Youth in Revolt: Five Powerful Movements Fueled by Young Activists," *National Geographic,* March 23, 2018.

5   Ibid.

6   Ibid.

because they already want a seat at the table. Most importantly, youth are comfortable with being uncomfortable. And they're okay with being uncomfortable in order to achieve comfort.

Now that was a bit. I hope you stayed with me through that metaphor there, but as we move forward in our world, as we become more diverse and more cognizant of the world, people, and systems around us, we are starting to see things through the lens of intersectionality. Youth see intersectionality as a foundation for making viable change.

Intersectionality is looking at a specific issue through several lenses, accounting for specific experiences, societal conflicts, and classist systems that people have been put through. "Intersectionality recognizes the idea that class, race, gender, sexual orientation, and disability do not exist separate from one another. Instead, they are deeply interwoven and even intersect for some marginalized groups of people."[7]

Youth are busy, sometimes busier than adults with school, extracurriculars, sports, and more. But youth have the time (and initiative) to learn about our societal systems, what's wrong with the world, and have the ability to contribute to daily, micro, and consistent change that builds up over time.

It might seem like I'm contradicting myself, but youth have decades to learn and advocate as they continue their

---

7   "What is intersectionality, and what does it have to do with me?" *YW Boston*, March 29, 2017.

lives. They also have tools that make making change easier and less time consuming than ever before, prompting more teens to do it. Right now, anyone has the opportunity to get on any social platform, start talking about issues or a particular set of issues that affect them or are important to them, and form a community and following out of their passion. The difference between other generations and Gen-Z is that *Gen-Z takes advantage of the opportunity to do so.*

Using social media is a daily opportunity to make change. And this might be micro, but change doesn't always have to be big. However, little actions, such as educating a member of one's community, can have ripple effects and change community values, legislation, and more.

In my experience, talking to even one person in a community that you are a part of, say a teacher at school or someone in your family, can lead to this very person talking to their network, and their network talking to their networks. Education can be powerful, and with people starting to support what you want to do, change is less impossible to implement.

Here's a personal example. I started a women's empowerment club at my high school. It seemed daunting at the time, as no student just "started" a club. But the more people I talked to about the importance of the club, the more research I did, and the more I emphasized how having the club could change the school for the better, the more support I garnered, which led to the establishment of the club.

"We are striking because we have done our homework and they have not."

— GRETA THUNBERG CLIMATE PROTEST IN

HAMBURG, GERMANY, MARCH 1, 2019 [8]

Young leaders now have the resources and ability to talk about something they care about.

Let that point sink in. There is no need to wait until a certain age to speak out. There is no more waiting until one has a degree or certain qualifications. Greta Thunberg, a global environmental activist, was fifteen years old when she called upon leaders to fight for the climate and fight for the world, and leaders answered. Greta is now a world leader, frequently seen at the United Nations and talking to some of the world's most prominent leaders, urging them to take steps to make our future sustainable.

But the Swedish teenager got started by skipping school to protest about climate change. That then led to her sitting outside the Swedish parliament every Friday to protest. By doing so, Greta singlehandedly called to action hundreds of thousands of world leaders to pay attention to the climate and the state of the future. As Greta said in her speech at the 2019 UN Youth Climate Summit in New York City, "We showed that we are united and that we, young people, are unstoppable."[9]

---

8   "Greta Thunberg quotes: 10 famous lines from teen activist," *BBC News,* September 25, 2019.

9   Hilary Brueck, "Greta Thunberg at UN Youth Climate Summit: 'We young people are unstoppable," *Insider News,* September 21, 2019.

This is a fundamental change from how activism and youth organizing used to take place because we don't need other people right away. Our voice is good enough and as long as we have the drive, we can take our stance to levels unbeknownst to even ourselves. And why wouldn't we?

"The eyes of all future generations are upon you."

—GRETA THUNBERG.10

Throughout history, what's the common thread that unites youth? A passionate, fiery desire to tear down and rebuild failed structures of the past. This desire can go in any direction. One of my friends, Sophia, is an indigenous Canadian youth who is suing her country's government. Sophia is one of fifteen plaintiffs suing the Canadian government for inaction on climate change. And Sophia isn't looking for financial reparations, but rather a long-term, well-thought-out climate plan based on the best available science and resources for her country to implement as soon as possible. As an indigenous youth, Sophia is a protector of the land and water. As her ancestors were, she is tasked to care for the land that she and her family live on and use every day. Sophia's story inspires me, but makes me think: Is what Sophia doing something anyone could have done even twenty years ago? Possibly, but not likely. Is it something that is more common today? Probably.

---

10   "Greta Thunberg tells world leaders 'you are failing us,' as nations announce fresh climate action," *United Nations Department of Economic and Social Affairs,* September 24, 2019.

This motivation and desire is also backed by science. Young people "between the ages of fourteen and twenty-nine show levels of generative (generativity is defined as concern for future generations as a legacy of the self) motivation that are as "high or even higher than adults,"[11] therefore underestimating the power of youth is a sheer mistake.

But you might be thinking, "I'm older than twenty-nine years old. What do I do?" Work with youth, for the world. Be an ally. Not only to youth activists, but to youth in general. As someone that is out of Gen-Z, you've been in the world for a while, which means you have access to resources and platforms that can be used to spotlight youth and their efforts in making change.

Also, empathize with Gen-Z. The issues of other generations manifest themselves for Gen-Z but amplified. What do I mean by that? For example, if you grew up as a white, female, Gen-Xer in the 1980s, you might feel insecure about your body or how you look, but maybe that means not getting a boyfriend as early or not being invited to parties in high school. For Gen-Z, this same body insecurity is perpetuated and amplified through social media, where a feed could be filled with skinny models that look perfect all the time (even though their photos are most likely heavily edited). You could get hate on your social media feed where everyone who follows you could see the hurtful comments of others, or never post any pictures because you overanalyze every single one of them. This might not seem like a big deal, but

---

11   Heather Lawford, *The Role of Attachment and Caregiving in the Emergence of Generativity from Early to Middle Adolescence*, (Concordia University, June 2008).

having body dysmorphia, coupled with an almost guaranteed imposter syndrome could lead to an eating disorder, or thoughts of self-harm, at a really early age. And this is a very basic example.

Millennials were named by TIME magazine as the "Me, Me, Me, Generation," and I'd say although Gen-Z has a selfish streak in which we will work for our own success, for the most part, we are a "We, We, We, Generation" who pushes for social change.[12]

"Almost 70 percent of young people are more fearful about tomorrow than hopeful. This is a really sobering statistic." This line was said by Ziad Ahmed at the DMEXCO conference, and just goes to show that *social good isn't a want anymore; it is a need.*[13]

Now, let's see where Gen-Z is in the midst of all this. Gen-Z doesn't stop and has few inhibitions. We're willing to take the first step and aren't waiting around for larger corporations to step up first. We will hold you accountable. Gen-Z has problem-solving and information-gathering skills beyond compare, and this leads to Gen-Z being well informed at a young age.

According to the *Digital Marketing Institute,* almost 90 percent of Gen-Zers spend part of their free time in activities they consider productive and creative, and almost 80 percent

---

12 Joel Stein, "Millennials: The Me Me Me Generation- Why Millennials will save us all," *Time Magazine,* May 20, 2013.

13 Ziad Ahmed speaking at *Digital Marketing Expo and Conference,* September 7- 8, 2021.

of them believe they will need to work harder than previous generations to succeed."[14]

Gen-Z has also lived through a lot. From being born around, or slightly before or after 9/11, being brought up in financial crisis, world turmoil and war, a global pandemic, and more, Gen-Z is used to being in crisis. Gen-Z is aware of what's going on around them and has a decision-making process that reflects that. Gen-Z feels responsible in general for the state of our future world, and places social good, ethical consumption, and social responsibility at the center of our endeavors and consumerism. We expect the same from companies and businesses that we support. In the following chapters, I will explore this assertion further through specific examples.

We also *cannot* be offline. You simply miss too much. And this is Riya Goel tested and approved, readers. I intentionally left my phone dead for twenty-four hours and didn't charge it so that I wouldn't log on to my phone. (Full disclosure: I couldn't go fully offline because I needed to do online school, so I needed access to a laptop; but I also didn't check any social media platform through my laptop.) I finally charged my phone the next day, and I was greeted with over five hundred notifications from all kinds of applications. Messages, Gmail, Instagram, Snapchat, TikTok, and more baited me with messages like "we missed you Riya!" or "hope you didn't forget about us..." but these notifications were right. In the twenty-four hours without

---

14   "Is Your Business Ready for the Rise of Generation Z?" *Digital Marketing Institute,* October 14, 2016.

logging on, I felt disconnected. I felt like I missed major updates, from acceptance letters to new relationships. But at the same time, I had a lot *more time*. Whether that meant talking to my best friend for another twenty minutes on a FaceTime call or reading a book for the first time in forever. So, take that information how you will. I'll explore all of this throughout the book.

Gen-Z has the social and technical skills to make a difference. Having grown up online, Gen-Z has an internalized filter that can pick up on a lack of authenticity, transparency, or poorly intended behaviors that don't resonate with the values of Gen-Z or what we want to see in a particular product or brand. Moving into the future, network and information spread are critical, and as we broaden our global networks through online interactions, this works to the advantage of Gen-Zers who have been online since we were young.

Chapter 2

Why Now?

Time is of the essence they say. I couldn't agree more. With technology, Gen-Z is able to make their time work for them by increasing productivity rates, creating big opportunities due to more free time, and doing more of what they love.

Big opportunities

Gen-Z is full of opportunity. We are all a few clicks away from changing the world, learning new skills and information, and making the next big thing—whether that be the next social media website, or leading the next social revolution. With this kind of accessibility, there are countless resources at one's fingertips that can be used to make a difference.

Gen-Z is able to take something that is "normal" in their lives, make it into a following, and take that very subject and form a community around it. TikTok, a short-form video app that gained popularity around 2019, has made ordinary people into full-time content creators. One of TikTok's very own shining stars is Sienna Mae Gomez. The body-positive icon has made videos and content surrounding body positivity.

By being able to create on a subject that others can resonate with, Sienna and others like her have been successful.

Sienna and other TikTokers who have risen to fame over a short period of time can speak to the fact that opportunity in today's day and age doesn't always mean being given something. It could simply be by chance, or by creating content based on an authentic subject matter that is meaningful to the creator. Later on, I will talk about the internal "BS filter" that Gen-Z has, and how part of the success of certain creators is passing this filter test that is so inherently built into Gen-Z.

The reason anyone and everyone can make it on social media is because there is no shortage of creatives that are making media more accessible and interactive. Even during the COVID lockdown, Gen-Z discovered and rocketed to popularity a previously niche form of content: podcasts. Julia Terpak, the founder of @genzconnect, says that, "Our generation is constantly consuming content. If there's a time you can't be looking down at your phone, then listening to it is the easiest way. For me, when I listen to podcasts, it feels like I'm actually learning rather than just scrolling through a feed continuously to see the same content recycled across platforms. That feels very mindless. With a podcast, it's similar to a book because you can get lost in the conversation and you feel like you are part of it. You feel like you're sitting in the room with these people. It's a totally different view."

Other apps, such as Houseparty, and games, such as AmongUs, also made their debut in the quarantine space for Gen-Z, as Gen-Z is constantly searching for ways to expand the media that we consume.

Going back to TikTok, something that popular creators collaborated on, as TikTok started to get more popular, were creator houses. And what are creator houses? Creator houses are essentially collaboration houses. Think about them like the HQ office of Facebook, or any other company for that matter. These houses, or mansions rather, are the "homes and headquarters for some of the top TikTok creators around."[15]

These houses are a strategic move for content creators. By having several creators under one roof, it is easier for users on a specific social media app or website to keep up with influencers or popular creators with large followings. This house model also allows for people to relate to and keep up with creators on social media platforms, which then gets users to keep consuming their content. JUV Consulting (whose CEO I got to interview... keep reading for some of his insights) came out with a trend report for Gen-Z in which they found that 48 percent of Gen-Z users reported that their willingness to keep up with influencers increased in 2020.[16]

Innovative thinking and collaboration are at the center of opportunity for Gen-Z. All it takes is some out-of-the-box thinking, and before you know it, your next video may go viral. With different methods of consumption available, opportunities to develop additional avenues for Gen-Z and

---

15   "Memes and Movements: 20 Trends that defined Gen Z in 2020," *JUV Consulting*, January 19, 202

16   Ibid.

future generations to consume content continue to present themselves.

Recognizing diversity matters.

Gen-Z is the most diverse generation to date. This is a common theme and has several benefits. Although race and color are still an issue in today's world, there is a greater desire for accessibility and opportunity for all, and Gen-Z recognizes this when they are put in positions of power.

Gen-Z knows that they need to make their workspaces inclusive and equitable, and that there is a need for equity not only in terms of race, but also in other scopes such as disability awareness, chronic diseases, and more. With more education and more resources available, Gen-Z is able to put themselves in the shoes of others, learn about the people that make up our world, and work toward making spaces where there is equal opportunity for all.

The world is changing by the minute in the digital sense, and Gen-Z is eager to learn and adapt to the changing environment. Seventy-six percent of Gen-Z professionals feel that the skills necessary in today's workforce are different from the skills necessary in past generations. Similarly, 91 percent of learning and development (L&D) leaders agree the skills necessary for today's workforce have changed, and the majority of Gen-Z (59 percent) don't feel their job will exist in the same form twenty years from now.[17] Learning such

---

17   Emily Poague, "Gen Z Is Shaping a New Era of Learning: Here's What you Should Know," *LinkedIn Learning Blog,* December 18, 2018.

skills and keeping up with the changing environment also adds financial incentive for Gen-Z that we don't turn down. Career advancement is easy as long as one can keep up, and this is important to Gen-Z.

Even though people might not agree with each other eye to eye, there is still acceptance of others and their views, opinions, and actions. Our generation has tolerance and acceptance not seen in other generations. You might be thinking, this doesn't really sound realistic. However, Gen-Z has been through a lot as a generation, and this has not only brought our generation together, but has taught Gen-Z what they hold valuable to them. Our experiences have almost given Gen-Z a moral compass of sorts. Collective trauma is something that I'll be talking about later on with pieces from my interview with Professor Dylan Miars of University of California, Berkeley.

There have been several defining experiences for Gen-Z already. Seeing police brutality on video or being able to watch an interview of someone who was assaulted allows for Gen-Z to understand the social constructs of our world at a different level than other generations past. We are able to see the "tough stuff" early on, and this forms our views for the future and makes us a generation who wants to work to right those wrongs.

With the technology, resources, and sheer power of our generation, this allows for immense opportunity moving forward. During the 2020 COVID outbreak, Gen-Z experienced a necessary call to action. From ACAB (All Cops Are Bad), to BLM (Black Lives Matter) protests, and even the capitol raids into the first few days of 2021, Gen-Z has seen unrest. Gen-Z knows unrest. Gen-Z wants to do something about unrest.

The answer to all of this? **Empathy.**

"Empathy is imbued in Generation Z's ethics, but we follow suit with action."[18] Despite living during a global pandemic in 2020 and 2021, Gen-Z showed up and out to call for reform in almost every single issue one could think of. From taking part in protests to so called "infographic activism," Gen-Z wants to educate themselves on what is going on around the world.

However, with limited exposure to the real world, and Gen-Z being fed information via social media, this task is daunting. There are, of course, flaws within approaches like infographic activism as well, where little to nothing results despite resharing and reposting information on social media. So where does that leave us? Demanding positions of power, and representation in offices of power where we can make viable change from the ground up.

"Gen-Z is not a monolith." This was one of the first things that Ziad Ahmed, the CEO of JUV Consulting, told me in our interview. Although Gen-Z is progressive, we represent a variety of political stances, viewpoints, and opinions. But we can generally bond around certain injustices. Quick case study: US Presidential election 2020; Settle for Biden.

Trump versus Biden. The final two candidates. The movement Settle for Biden was founded by youth that formerly rallied

---

18   Ibid.

behind candidates Elizabeth Warren and Bernie Sanders. These two progressive candidates had to end their campaigns, but the youth who supported them weren't finished. Although youth weren't ecstatic about the Biden campaign and Joe Biden being the Democratic presidential candidate, anything was better than Trump for most of Gen-Z.

This birthed Settle for Biden, or @settleforbiden online. This account, run by teenagers from across the United States, created content and infographics online to help rally behind Biden. Although I'm no election expert, I can say I'm fairly certain the efforts of Settle for Biden helped to contribute to Joe Biden securing the position of President of the United States.

But this account did more than just get Biden into the White House. What it really did is show people the power of youth coming together, and more specifically, Gen-Z youth. This account, and many others, like @soyouwantotalkabout, have countless reposts on social media platforms like Instagram and Twitter, leading to the popularity of online activism, further empowering Gen-Z to take a stance on what matters to them.

This is a long section. But here's my last bit. The most important diversity that Gen-Z has to offer? **Diversity of thought.**

Let's look at TikTok (again, I know). The platform (which I will explain in the next chapter more in depth) has several "sides." This could be fashion, cooking, spirituality, or really anything for that matter. But what makes Gen-Z unique is being open to these sides of TikTok. I skeptically downloaded TikTok in the middle of quarantine, around July 2020. My little sister had the app before I did and would spend hours on it. Being the wise and sensible person I thought myself to be, I tried playing with a little self-control and invested my time in other things. Eventually, I caved and downloaded the application. After I did, I never went back.

Although I can say with full confidence I spend more time on TikTok than I do any other application, I learn so much more on the app in comparison to other platforms. From learning how to style different clothing items, or how to invest my money in the stock market, TikTok has it all. And the diversity of content that we are able to consume, on just one application, speaks to the diversity of Gen-Z. Of course, there are downsides of TikTok's for-you page, which I will explore later. However, TikTok is Gen-Z's platform, and says a lot about its primary audience.

Because of this diversity in thought and exposure to new ideas, Gen-Z can make up a mind of their own. Seen in the 2020 US presidential election even, Gen-Zers found themselves with parents who were Republican Trump supporters with kids who were #settlingforBiden. In a normal world, this sheer divide in a family would be almost impossible to deal with.

However, Gen-Z can find a home in online spaces. Spaces online are where Gen-Zers can come together, find people in similar situations, and educate themselves about how to deal with the situations that they are facing. These online spaces can feel like safe havens when physical spaces and gatherings aren't always possible. And online creators facilitate such spaces to an extent. Creators that are, for example, politically inclined, teach their following about global issues, or the importance of local elections, and raise importance to such issues.

Personally, online spaces have been a godsend. I never felt like people in my high school or many people from my area understood what I wanted to do, or what I wanted to work on. Online spaces gave me a chance to be myself for once and interact with people who thought the way that I did and supported me through my endeavors.

Power of this generation

Gen-Z has an immense amount of power, and we are anything but a monolith. In addition to being the most diverse generation, we are also the largest generation to date. Now, largest generation to date means something. It means that as Gen-Z starts to become consumers, our spending power is going to be colossal, meaning that brands *have* to pay attention to us. There is no way that one can *ignore* Gen-Z or go around Gen-Z, because the impact that we will assert on the world is going to stay—at least for a little while.

An Analysis of #genz

Okay. So, to prove that Gen-Z is worth your time, I've done a simple search. I've typed in #genz on five different platforms: Instagram, TikTok, LinkedIn, Twitter, and YouTube. I also obviously checked Google. Here's what I found.

P.S. (I logged out of all of my social media accounts in order to search #genz. As I will talk about later on, social media platforms show users content based on their interests and what they want to see. I'm interested in Gen-Z and different intersections of Gen-Z, and so I didn't want my search results to be influenced by my interactions on social media)

Instagram: On Instagram, the search yielded over 335,000 posts, the top of which included posts from accounts @soyouwanttotalkabout and @zenerations (whose executive director I will be talking to later on in the book). Instagram was the birthplace for online infographic-style activism which showcased the power of Gen-Z. Of course, this hashtag would not be complete without the occasional meme (an idea, behavior, or style that becomes a fad and spreads by means of imitation from person to person within a culture and often carries symbolic meaning representing a particular phenomenon or theme) describing Gen-Z.

TikTok: TikTok is different. #genz has 3.4 billion views. Not million, BILLION. This goes to show that TikTok is Gen-Z's platform and has found a special place in almost every Gen-Zer's heart during the global pandemic. From the top ten videos underneath the hashtag on TikTok, I got a lot. I watched a video about a girl, @abby_gillmer, who wrote a poem on Gen-Z and how we are being taught under the current education system, being forced to memorize information that is irrelevant in the real world, and not learning relevant, real-world skills like resume building or how to buy a car. This video ended with the line, "education is teaching us how to hate the thing we love most: learning."[19]

But then there were videos, like by verified creator @brittany.xavier, who made a video about acting like her Gen-Z daughter, down to Gen-Z language, mannerisms, and even including bits about producing content and online school. Then there were videos about Gen-Zers saying how they

---

19   Abby Gillmer (@abby_gillmer), TikTok video.

wouldn't give their kids iPads and iPhones early on (more about that later). I also watched several POV (point of view) videos where Gen-Zers acted as if they were doctors, lawyers, etc., with Gen-Z sayings and actions.

Finally, there were videos that spoke to the true nature of Gen-Z. From the change that we've created by calling out what's wrong without any inhibitions, such as spamming the comments section of a president's recent social media posts, or that of a serial killer in order to demand justice, to the distrust that we have in the media because we can't believe everything that we read online. There are even videos on how Gen-Z has the tendency of turning to comedy under duress, and the competition we have with each other for everyone's attention online.

So, TikTok was a lot. It was transparent but gave me a good idea of what Gen-Z is (and is one of the main resources I turned to in writing this book).

LinkedIn: Of course, LinkedIn doesn't primarily have a Gen-Z audience. But, the fact that this hashtag exists on the platform has meaning. On LinkedIn, around two thousand and five hundred people follow #genz, but I have to mention, there are other iterations of the hashtag that have following as well, such as #genzmarketing and #genzs. However, a lot more people would be able to see the posts with #genz in them based on connections.

Anyways, LinkedIn was interesting. At the top of the hashtag was JUV Consulting, with their consistent posting about who Gen-Z is and what we're about. (I get to talk to the CEO,

Ziad Ahmed, later on in the book.) I see people talking about Gen-Zers in the workspace, and what that might look like. I see one of my friends, Sophie Beren of the Conversationalist, being featured on goodgigs. I see people outside of Gen-Z asking those that are a part of Gen-Z to help them out in terms of catering their businesses and business models to the new generation. I hope I can help with that.

Twitter: On the top of the hashtag, (meaning people who liked and shared certain posts the most using the Gen-Z hashtag) I found a group of teens having a modeling photoshoot for their new band, a couple of teens coming together to form a company, and a couple people from other generations posting about their kids or relatives that were a part of Gen-Z and the accomplishments that such individuals had achieved at such a young age, such as buying a house at the age of twenty or paying their parents' bills because of the financial status that they had attained.

YouTube: After TikTok got popular, YouTube has been filled with TikTok compilations that describe a certain characteristic or topic. This is the same with Gen-Z. The first search results I got were TikTok compilations of "typical behaviors" of Gen-Z. Then I saw Millennial versus Gen-Z videos, where a member of each generation would assess or talk about a topic or a set of objects. This was interesting to me, as many people find it hard to draw the line between Gen-Z and Millennials sometimes, especially in the area of overlap around those that were born in the last decade of the 1900s. I also found videos on Gen-Z terminology and Gen-Z's takes on issues like socialism, the environment, and gender inequality.

Google: Google was general. It gave me a general understanding of who Gen-Z is and provided links to articles and statistics like that of Pew Research (of which I took a few). Among the links that are listed on the Gen-Z search, there are several comparison links putting Gen-Z up against other generations, links to Twitter threads, a great Business Insider study on Gen-Z, and also research and data about Gen-Z from large companies and tech giants like Dell, Deloitte, and Touche.

This caught my attention and also poses the question: why aren't people that are in Gen-Z talking about Gen-Z? The average employee age at Deloitte and Touche is forty, and the average at Dell is around thirty-five. These people aren't in Gen-Z. I figured, let's hear about Gen-Z from a Gen-Zer.

So, what was this for? I wanted to do this analysis, or explanation for that matter, to show how different platforms garner different results and content even for the same search. This is one of the reasons why Gen-Zers have so many social platforms on their devices. I also wanted to give you an overview of what is to come in the next few chapters, so stay tuned.

The internet to Gen-Z, and the world really, is the greatest tool out there. In seconds, one can get an answer to a multivariable calculus problem (okay, maybe that's only specific to my use), but in all seriousness, anyone can learn anything with the internet, and very easily as well. Growing up on the internet, Gen-Zers are almost the guinea pigs of the internet world, downloading social media around elementary school to middle school on their devices. But this provides us with a salient knowledge of how to use the internet and the resources available to us to our advantage. This allows us to become more lucrative with our passions and know how to capitalize on areas of interest rather than having to go into corporate or government jobs like our parent's generation.

The internet presents almost endless opportunity for Gen-Z, such as being able to connect and chat with a CEO on LinkedIn or get on an Instagram live with a world leader ready to rally with youth. This is power. And this very power allows us to speak up and act upon injustices that we have witnessed since almost the day we were born. This is what makes Gen-Z different.

Futurism: a concern with events and trends of the future, or which anticipate the future. [20]

The right hashtag, using the right audio on a video, or even saying the right thing, could lead to a video going viral, which means several thousands of shares within a short period of time. In the future, Gen-Z will play a large role in determining trends to come (as they do already). Being able to accurately predict something that will potentially become a trend will prove to be beneficial in terms of numbers on social media. More likes, shares, and comments on a video means more money coming to the creator, the more brand exposure a particular creator gets, and this opens up opportunities for creators as well. So, futurism in the future is going to lead to more opportunities.

A lot of the future is up to Gen-Z. As a generation, we lack a lot of in-person interaction. And this isn't really our faults.

---

20   *Oxford Languages, Lexico.* s.v. "futurism (n.)" Accessed Feb 26, 2021.

We were handed devices very young. We are living through a global pandemic when online "Zoom school" is the only way to get an education. This in-person interaction, however, is something that our generation longs for.

At the beginning of the pandemic in 2020, and even currently, there is sentiment online expressing how Gen-Z is almost jealous of other generations for not having to be exposed to the world so quickly and being shielded from trauma. Gen-Z wants to be able to experience the world, have fun with friends, and not always be online. Videos have been circulating on how Gen-Zers don't want to give their children iPads and iPhones as stated earlier. This means that although being online is crucial for Gen-Z, we might not want to spend our lives on it 24/7, and that ideology will be present in some way, shape, or form in areas in which we innovate in the future.

Chapter 3

Now, let's look at this more closely

———

Gen-Z has a lot going on. From tech, to politics, to school, and more, there is a lot happening underneath the umbrella of Gen-Z. This section? Call it a mental break. Take a breather and brace yourself for the main chunk of this book.

Here are some big ideas that will be explored more deeply in the next few chapters:

- Access to resources
- Gen-Z being hyperconnected and having a global network
- Talk to us, not about us!
- We have a desire to be better; there are so many things we need to do for a better world
- Living with a set of collective traumas, and we need to bridge generations
- We all have our unique talents, so why not use the resources available to do what we want to do?

These common themes are going to be supported by interviews from people in diverse fields, including Gen-Zers that are defining the world today.

And, here's an introduction.

What makes this book unique? My perspective embedded into all that I'm writing about. I am a Gen-Zer and being within the generation I'm writing about gives me a unique vantage point that I want to share. Throughout the book, I'll be incorporating some of my own personal stories to show how the insights I'm sharing manifest in a Gen-Zer's life. So, I thought that it was only appropriate that you got to know a little bit about me before I move on into the biggest section of the book.

Hi. I'm Riya Goel. Right now, I'm a senior at West Orange High School in New Jersey. Not sure where I'll be when you read this, but that's where I started. I like to call myself an intersectional feminist. So, if you read the word "intersect" or "intersectionality" a lot, apologies in advance. I'm an advocate at heart, starting a co-ed, varsity, fencing team, Meatless Mondays program, and women's empowerment club at my high school. I've been a teen advisor at Girl Up, Girl Advocate at the Working Group on Girls to the United Nations, and researcher at the Princeton Student Climate initiative, so far. I've started organizations, initiatives, and projects of my own, rallied around my community, and much more, but you can see that on my social media. My purpose in introducing myself is to share why I have the perspective that I convey throughout this book. As a Gen-Zer, I believe that my generation has the tools and drive necessary to make change, and I want to show you why.

Part II

What's so unique about us (with stories, of course!) and how does Gen-Z do things differently?

Chapter 4

Tech, Tech. And more tech

___

We know everything about technology because we've grown up with it. Technology is like second nature to Gen-Z, and it has literally rocked our world. Growing up when technology was taking off means that we know the ins and outs, how stuff works, and how to #hackthesystem. We also create amazing inventions, programs, and more that make our lives easier (or harder in some cases) on the daily. This presents itself as three notions for our generation: a built-in BS filter from being online 24/7, community, and opportunity. Though they present as completely independent concepts, they in fact are equally important and function as part of a greater experience for Gen-Z.

"We have never had the luxury of ignorance," writes Nadya Okamoto (who I'll be talking to later on in this section)."We are either personally impacted by what's happening around us, or know someone who is, so the effect of the crisis is much closer to us, and we feel empowered to do something about it."[21] This is why we want to make change online, and why we want to make sure it lasts.

Our internal BS filter

Let's talk about the BS filter that Gen-Z so innately has. And, let's revisit Ava McDonald.

Ava McDonald is a force to be reckoned with. Not only is she a CEO at just eighteen years old, but with her company, Zfluence, she has tapped into the ten-billion-dollar-a-year market of Instagram marketing and economy. Ava, an incoming freshman at Georgetown University in 2020, was inspired to create Zfluence when she came across generic and clearly pre-planned "copy-pasted" captions that influencers on Instagram included with items they promoted via paid partnerships. Ava said that "she could totally see through it." She could easily identify which posts demonstrated that influencers truly loved the brand or product they were promoting, and posts in which the relationship and brand partnership was clearly a monetary partnership.

With 70 percent of teenagers trusting influencers more than celebrities, Ava saw how her friends were "taking product recommendations" from influencers via the products they were promoting. She saw an opportunity in this and asked the essential question: "Why shouldn't my friends and I be able to benefit from the really cool marketing economy that's happening on Instagram right now?"

---

21   Nadya Okamoto, "Generation Z: A Generation of Distrust and Disruption," *Advertising Week 360*, September 10, 2019.

Throughout talking to Ava, she always came back to "authenticity," and the importance of this in our technology-driven world. With social media completely changing the consumer landscape and providing opportunities for anyone doing, quite literally, anything to go viral and to succeed, there has been no shortage of "fluff" content and an exaggeration of the truth on such social networks. However, Gen-Z, being on social networks their entire lives, has almost a sixth sense when it comes to weeding out what is true and what is false on their feeds.

Ava identified this need and wanted to create a network of "Z-fluencers" that would promote products in exchange for product, and not money. The idea is that this will ensure that the influencer, no matter how big or small, is promoting something that they truly love and use instead of being motivated by a monetary incentive. Ava mentioned how some influencers are so clearly only after the money and not the product that some celebrities and influencers have "accidentally posted the entire email as their caption, like hey x let's have you post the below caption thanks, you'll be receiving your check in the mail," exposing the true nature of the relationship between the brand and influencer.

When I asked Ava what she thinks sets Gen-Z apart from other generations, she immediately said that "we don't have as much avocado toast as Millennials." But Ava is right. Where Millennials and older generations were exposed to social media later in their lives, Gen-Z has grown up with technology their whole lives, being exposed to the internet from the day they are born. We're more authentic in our interactions, showing off more of our day-to-day life compared to the curated, perfect feeds of Millennials, sometimes exclusively for avocado toast. We also don't buy into as many frivolous trends as Millennials, and Gen-Z trends are more centered around everyday happenings and occurrences.

Millennials and other generations generally have different uses for social media, whether this be networking or sharing life updates. For most of Gen-Z, social media is their life, with Gen-Zers spending an average of ten hours surfing the web every single day.[22]

The most used social media platforms between Gen-Z and Millennials also differ, with Gen-Z mainly using Instagram, YouTube, Snapchat, and recently TikTok, whereas Millennials, who started their social media journeys on applications like Tumblr, Pinterest, and MySpace now spend the majority of their time on Twitter, Instagram, Facebook, and LinkedIn. But within these two generations, Instagram is in the middle of the Venn diagram, catering to both older generations and new users joining every day. This is what makes this platform so powerful and what places Instagram at the forefront of influencer marketing, with this broad audience that encompasses people from all walks of life.

With Gen-Z spending so much time on their phones, mobile devices, and computers, we shift away from the facade of social media perpetuated by Millennials. We are no longer expected or required to portray a perfect life, where we only

---

22 Colm Hebblethwaite, "Gen Z engaging with 10 hours of online content a day," *Marketing Tech,* February 9, 2018.

share vacation moments, or where we get our next trendy latte. Rather, we desire a more authentic, casual, and realistic picture, with Gen-Z tackling hard topics like mental health and sexual assault on their personal accounts.

Ava emphasized how "Gen-Z is really taking charge in a way that Millennials haven't with social media, where they're posting more about what they believe and less about traveling or getting lattes." This aligns perfectly with what Ava is doing professionally; people are able to post about products that they authentically love.

Ava explained that although Gen-Z follows the precedent that Millennials have set, they operate through another lens. "By being able to share things that you love with social media, you're sharing what you're doing, what kind of products you're into, what restaurants you are going to, and more." So, instead of fitting in, the concept of social media has been to display your own authenticity. This allows for "less of a presentational aesthetic of something that is authentically you."

When I asked Ava about what she thought resonated with Gen-Z, she discussed the notions of inclusivity, authenticity, and sustainability. She talked about how Gen-Z has a need to perform social good, whether this be performative or genuine, although Ava and many other Gen-Zers can usually tell the difference between the two. Ava explained the importance of "people being able to use social media as a way to organize and to share their beliefs and connect with people."

"As a generation we're doing a really great job to make sure that everybody's voices are being heard and to be as inclusive and diverse as possible." Gen-Z values diversity and sees that more industries need to diversify and include a range of voices and experiences.

Ava continued that "Gen-Z has already had so much impact as a group, and the number of movements, events, and more that we've organized and put together is just crazy to think about." She talked about how she reads about other Gen-Z founders, CEOs, and people who are doing innovating with their time. Ava talked about how being a part of this generation of change makers is inspiring.

If there are two things that one can take from this interview, one is truly the fact that age doesn't matter anymore. In order to get the support of Gen-Z, influencers and companies have to a) use the platforms Gen-Z are actually on and b) post inclusive and authentic content. Teens are doing everything and anything, from starting their own companies, consulting firms, fashion brands, and lifestyle brands before even graduating high school or college. Ava said that her age "is her biggest strength," and being so young is both an opportunity and a struggle.

Gen-Z values diversity and sees that more industries need to diversify and include a range of voices and experiences in their marketing. Many older generations underestimate and undervalue the skillsets, knowledge, and commitment that young people from Gen-Z possess. However, to the contrary, there are also brands that take the opportunity to hire and invest in youth, that are often more successful. As Ava said, "brands that want to listen to voices from our generation, and who are able to take the authentic firsthand feedback that I'm able to provide is my biggest strength and to their advantage, because I understand Gen-Z firsthand just from being part of it."

If there is one thing that Ava radiates, it is a need for authenticity in an increasingly technology-based world, where being inauthentic might be easier than just being you.

Here are three quotes from Ava to sum this bit up:
- "Focus on authentic relationships, which then results in the most compelling and influential social media posts."
- "I think that we have a really powerful ability to be the influencers, who are actually able to market products. Authenticity is so important to us and it's the number one driving force in our purchasing decisions and just the way we live our lives."
- "My age is my biggest strength."

This is what Ava and Zfluence are all about, and what is important to Gen-Z.

We take tech with a grain of salt... and it's evident

We have a distrust in the media and don't believe everything that we read online. But our lives are on the internet too, so we're in this sort of paradox where we're still trying to figure out and establish our relationship with our devices and the role that they play in our lives.

We are constantly scrolling through content every day, which includes content with warnings and labels on how information could be inaccurate, and the notion of #FakeNews being perpetuated everywhere, even by a former president of the United States. This makes us, Gen-Zers, question our trust in the government, large companies and corporations, and people in power. After all, we've been raised in the so-called "post-truth era," where there's so much false information out there that sometimes even the truth doesn't seem so real.

"Perhaps what you could call a coping mechanism to this collective distrust is Generation Z's turn to memes—our own art of reactionary, humorous, extremely replicable visual content. For many younger members of Generation Z, meme groups are one of the final reasons to still have a Facebook account."[23]

Memes, in tandem with other jokes online, contribute to Gen-Z's sense of self-deprecating humor. This might sound unhealthy, but in reality, it's a way for Gen-Z to cope with everything that is going on around us and feel a sense of togetherness in such behaviors and jokes. This self-deprecation also adds to our self-awareness, where we overanalyze ourselves and strive for perfection, or our perceived definition of perfection.

There is also the issue of misinformation with 59 percent of Gen-Z finding out what is going on in the world through social media. With "everyone wanting to be heard, provoking a reaction is seen as a political statement in and of itself."[24]

---

23 Ibid.
24 Kate Taylor, "Gen Z is more conservative than many realize — but the Instagram-fluent generation will revolutionize the right," *Business Insider, The State of Gen-Z.*

So, what does this mean exactly? We're not sure where we stand with all the information out there. Sometimes it's hard to fact-check the information that we're viewing online, and a lot of times, we're stuck in echo chambers of our own opinions, which makes it even harder to understand if our views and the information that we're receiving is accurate or not. However, we want to work on a more inclusive, authentic, and factual internet space where #fakenews is a thing of the past.

A quick dive into what's on my computer.
Now that you know a little bit about me, I have a million things to do. And this isn't unique to me at all. So, on my laptop at any given point, I generally have:
- Two browsers open (Safari and Chrome)
  - each with about three windows
  - each window having around ten to twenty tabs
- Text messaging
- Zoom (during classes/meetings)
- the Notes app for reminders/to-do lists
- Slack
- Spotify
- and more

Why is this relevant?

I can never stay focused—at least not for long if I'm being completely transparent. Honestly, it's impossible. If I wanted to do my calculus homework for example, I might need two tabs open at most, one tab with the assignment, and maybe another for formulas or notes from class. However, I probably couldn't really do just calculus for more than ten minutes straight, because I'd get a text notification, or I might go look at my Instagram or email. I might even have a scholarship application that I totally forgot about that is a tab on this window that also has the tabs to complete my calculus homework. There are always distractions, and it's really hard to stay focused with everything that is open at one time on my computer.

And what's on everyone's computer differs. Some people might have gaming programs, music, recording, Photoshop, and more open at a given point as well.

We're different people online and find solace in that.

We're different online. The fact of the matter is that if you met me in person, I'd seem relatively introverted and almost in my own bubble sometimes. However, online, I'm outgoing and am not afraid to speak out or post about something that I care about. This is the same story with a lot of other Gen-Zers, who in person, don't show their true talents, or "sides" until they reveal themselves online. From hidden makeup artists to secret stock market fanatics, the internet almost acts as a level playing field where the opportunity is endless, and all you need to do is create. This provides Gen-Zers with an escape—an escape from reality, the struggles of daily life, and just stress in general. That's also one of the reasons why being online is so addicting.

But, not all of it is good...

Online, we build a self-image that we can fall in love with. But sometimes, we fall in love with an image of ourselves that we're not. Oftentimes with filters, and editing tools online, we don't look like our pictures that we post on social media.

We alter our own image to look better on a feed. So, a lot of what we do is for face value.

We're also privy to constant surveillance. If your accounts online are public, anyone can find your profile and see what you're doing or sharing. We're also able to see who watches us—who likes our content—so we're always being watched. That's not only scary, but more so, it's hard to keep up with. This leads to Gen-Z being hypersensitive, because we can be shamed or commented on at any moment in time.

The manifestation of aesthetics

Through our online personalities, we've collectively developed certain aesthetics that can be found online, like cottagecore, e-boys/girls, dark academia, bruh girls, kidcore, softcore, and more. These aesthetics are a collection of sorts of ideas, outfits, behaviors, slang, and activities that certain groups of people take part in. For example, cottagecore was something that rose in popularity as TikTok started to become the primary platform for Gen-Zers. Cottagecore has elements of gardens, fresh fruits, meadows, and a life in the countryside. These aesthetics provide Gen-Zers with an escape, where they can truly imagine what they would be interested in if societal expectations, birthed circumstances, and survival weren't a priority.

Sides of TikTok, explained

Ever thought of the word niche outside of the context of a biology classroom? Okay, maybe that joke wasn't my best, but the key word here is: niche. Niches are specialized subject matter, skills, etc., around which content creators can center their content to build a specific audience that is interested in that content due to their shared interest in a specific niche.

On the surface, TikTok is full of dance videos, but what makes the platform special is its almost too specific algorithm that boasts the For-You Page, or FYP, for each user on the platform. Each user's FYP is a "curation of audios, trends, and creators suited to users' tastes." Ever the label-loving cohort, Generation-Z has taken to naming different "sides" of TikTok, with "straight TikTok" being the most mainstream form of content such as dancing and lip-syncing videos. But if you find yourself in Alt-TikTok, you'll become acquainted with a whole new set of trends and creators that drive this select niche.

Sides of TikTok are unique because they engage users based on their interests. They allow users to connect and engage with others all over the world who are interested in the same things they are, no matter how unique.

Want to try thinking of sides of TikTok that might be a fit for you? Here are some of the most popular sides of TikTok, from most popular to least popular, according to JUV consulting.

- Comedy
- Alt (alternative)
- Fashion
- Political
- Queer
- Indie
- Food/Cooking
- Messy
- Conspiracy
- Travel
- Prison
- Dog/Pet
- Interior design

- Frog
- Stock/Business
- Straight
- Ban/Cancel
- Rap[25]

Think one or more of these sides is a fit for you? I know that my FYP is filled with multiple sides of TikTok, all personalized for me via the algorithm.

The For-You Page is probably the most unique aspect of the TikTok platform. Based on how one interacts with a particular video (such as liking the video, commenting, or sharing it to another person), the TikTok algorithm is able to assess what kind of content one likes to consume, creating the For-You Page, content tailored by an algorithm, for you. This mechanism of the algorithm leads to the creation of "sides" of TikTok. There is a "straight" side to TikTok with primarily cis creators, whereas there are also sides like "political" TikTok, or "black" TikTok, where one is able to see a lot of content that falls under such categories based off of their interactions with other videos. This contributes to how addictive TikTok is because it provides you with content that you want to see and are genuinely interested in.

We're different on each platform.
Interestingly enough, we are also different people based on the particular social platform that we are on. "A new study from Pennsylvania State University finds that many social

---

25 "Memes and Movements: 20 Trends that defined Gen Z in 2020," *JUV Consulting*, January 19, 2020.

media users tweak the way they come off on different platforms for one simple reason—they just want to fit in."[26]

This concept might sound insane, and could remind you of multi-personality disorder, but in reality, it makes sense. An individual who might be posting a picture of their new outfit on Instagram or Snapchat, might then write an article about the impact of fast fashion and post this on their LinkedIn. This is because we all have several social platforms. What sets us apart on each of these platforms is simple: we convey different messages about ourselves on each platform.

Community

Community is apparent in the Gen-Z world. And you might be thinking, community means meeting people, interacting with people, and doing things in real life (IRL)! I'd argue that you can do all that and more online. During the coronavirus quarantine of 2020 and 2021, this has become more apparent as everyone can see the countless ways in which we are interacting with each from the comfort of our homes. Gen-Z has created a virtual world where you can connect to anyone, and you might even find people on the other side of your country or across oceans who think just like you.

Community can also be fostered on social networks like TikTok.

---

26   Chris Opfer, "Our Online Personalities Change Across Different Social Media Platforms." *How Stuff Works,* May 27, 2017.

With an impeccably created FYP that sometimes hits a little too close to home, the platform features short videos no longer than one minute on the application to share diverse content, from dance videos to a conversation about a political stance. The diversity of TikTok is what makes it so unique for Gen-Z. TikTok makes it so easy to become a creator, and finding your audience isn't hard with the FYP.

Many companies have started to use TikTok as a platform to reach Gen-Z, and this has shifted marketing strategies, with more companies choosing to use "TikTok stars" as their ambassadors versus actors and well-known individuals. This can be seen with Charli and Dixie D'Amelio, two teenage sisters who are the top creators on the app with over ninety-four million followers and forty-one million followers respectively. The sister pair has landed some pretty amazing opportunities for a girl who just graduated high school and another who will in two years. The sisters have paired up with Morphe to create the Morphe 2 line of makeup, and are also Hollister jean representatives, designing and creating their own pairs of jeans.[27][28]

Dixie D'Amelio has also been able to release her song, "Happy," and got the opportunity to collaborate with stars Blackbear and Lil Mosey. Charli has her own drink at Dunkin Donuts (which you may have already gotten the chance to order) and has even worked with UNICEF on a campaign to wash hands during one of the peaks of the coronavirus. This TikTok

27 Charli D'amelio (@charlidamelio) account on TikTok, Accessed February 27, 2021.
28 Dixie D'amelio (@dixiedamelio) account on TikTok, Accessed February 27, 2021.

success is not just limited to these sisters. One of their friends, Addison Rae, signed to represent American Eagle Jeans and launched her own beauty line, Item Beauty. What started as simple dance videos with their friends turned these three girls into international superstars, with followings larger than the populations of some countries.

With this in mind, several creators capitalize on a particular theme or set of messages in their content to drive up their success rates. These sides of TikTok also contribute to the community aspect of the app, where one can find people that think like them and form bonds online that are everlasting.

TikTok is not only a platform to dance and have fun with. There is also some serious advocacy, activism, political action, and real conversation happening on TikTok. Since videos can "blow up" fast due to the success of the FYP, it isn't uncommon for videos to reach a large amount of people.

It is extremely easy to be dismissive of the application, but the truth of the matter is that you might be behind if you aren't on the app. Personally, I didn't get the app until mid-quarantine, around June of 2020. There were songs and terms that I had no idea about prior to getting the app, which I finally understood once I got on the app.

With TikTok having such a large audience, and videos having potential to reach a large number of people quickly, the music industry has also jumped on TikTok as a platform to easily promote their music. If a creator creates a dance to a song that goes viral, most creators will jump on the trend, and post videos with the music on their videos. Even large presences like Jennifer Lopez and Bebe Rexha have enlisted A-listers on the app like Charli D'Amelio to create dances to their music in hopes of this inciting a larger movement around their music, leading to more views of their videos, more plays of the song, more success, and more monetary profit at the end of the day.

With the videos on TikTok being so short, this enables an easy spread of information. Trends come and go with the information on the application moving so fast.

What makes platforms like TikTok so successful is the **power of relatability** that comes with it. When people are able to relate to content, it generally makes that content more successful and powerful in terms of bringing everyone together.

Gen-Z is used to the fast pace of the internet, and we can make something new out of anything we're given. Gen-Z is the definition of opportunity, and this is only possible through technology.

Chapter 5

Yup... tech has its downsides

____

Overall, this book is very tech positive, but I'd be remiss to not discuss its downsides. Such drawbacks can be avoided and moderated, but here are some common ones to be aware of:

- The race to get verified
- Instant gratification
- Imposter syndrome
- Cancel culture
- Blurred line between work and home
- Lack of soft, social skills
- Multitasking and burnout
- Mental health issues
- Lack of authenticity
- Why Gen-Zers won't be giving our kids iPads and iPhones early on
- The movie: *The Social Dilemma*

The race to get verified

We compete for people's attention, and then we tie that attention to our self-worth. Even I've been one to chase after my follower count in an attempt to get verified. But the reality is, getting verified or trying to have a large following is not always worth it, and here's why.

First, let's look at the psychology behind likes

We curate our lives around this perceived sense of perfection because we are rewarded in the short term with hearts, likes, or thumbs up on our social media accounts. We conflate these likes with value and truth, but the reality is that this fake and frankly brutal popularity makes you think, "what can I do better to get more attention?" And this question can lead people to take part in activities that they wouldn't normally do.

"A recent study on the effect social media likes have on a teenagers brain liken it to winning money or eating chocolate. The study also demonstrated that people are more likely to engage with posts that have been endorsed/liked by a large amount of their peers—a follow the crowd mentality. That little rush you get when your post gets more likes than normal? There is a reason for that rush. Dopamine. For every thumb up or heart we receive, we get a little psychological high through a shot of dopamine. The more likes the more shots. The more shots we have, the more shots we want. And we're in a loop. Scientists used to think dopamine was responsible for pleasure in the brain, but we now know that rather than create pleasure it makes us seek it.

It's come to a point where we treat likes as a method of determining social standing. "By posting online, you're making yourself vulnerable to the thoughts of others. If the post doesn't elicit the reaction you'd hoped for, it can hurt."[29]

Here's some facts on how being online affects Gen-Z

- US hospital admission for non-fatal self-harm in teenage girls was stable until around 2010 when it started rising around 62 percent since 2009 for girls ages fifteen to nineteen and 189 percent (nearly triple) from girls ages ten to fourteen and has kept going up since. Suicide is up 70 percent and 151 percent and that pattern points to social media.[30]
- Gen-Z is the first generation that got on social media in middle school or earlier. We come home and go straight to our devices, not outside to play or anything of that nature. In fact, toys sales have gone down, specifically ever since the close of retailer ToysRUS in 2018. "While there are a lot of factors at 'play,' a big part of the issue is that the Batmobiles and Barbie dolls have been gathering dust in the rec room as children's faces are lit by glowing apps and bleeping video games. Now when you type into Google, 'My kid is addicted to…' the top suggested word to fill in the blank is 'Minecraft,' followed by sugar, then Xbox, then 'Roblox,' another block-building game. That's right, Minecraft is more addictive than sugar, according to what people are anxiously typing into Google."[31]

29 "The Psychology of Being 'Liked' on Social Media," *Start Digital*, November 27, 2017.
30 Ibid.
31 Ben Popken, "Did Video Games and iPads Kill Toys R Us?" *NBC News*, September 19, 2017.

- Gen-Z is more anxious, fragile and stressed, and much less comfortable taking risks. So, in a sense, we're becoming more conservative. How can we see this? The rates at which we're getting our driver's licenses are going down, and the number of dates we go on is going down too.
  - Speaking of dates. Gen-Z has a lack of trust in our relationships, which leads to the whole dating and relationship scheme for our generation being very different. With apps like Tinder, we aren't required to commit to anything. Such apps allow us to have *short-term, no commitment* relationships. Why? Because if one "match" doesn't end up working out, we know there's a thousand other options on the app that might be better than the last. These kinds of interactions make breaking relationships extremely easy, no strings attached.
  - But still, why are we really conservative with our actions or sharing on social media? Because we've seen the effects of the bad. We've seen where a picture meant for one person ends up on the screens of a million others, or where one comment can get someone canceled.
- We have a *digital pacifier* that is atrophying our own ability to deal with what we want.
- There is a notion that we can adapt, but tech is now growing *exponentially* and not gradually to which our brains haven't evolved yet.

Instant gratification
Being online our whole lives, Gen-Z is used to getting everything relatively quickly. When extensive work is required in

order to achieve something, this expectation can act as somewhat of a deterrent for Gen-Z. We are not willing to do something that we are not 100 percent interested in unless there is a good enough reason to do so. Gen-Z's need for instant gratification presents itself in the social networks that we call our favorites, like TikTok, where our attention is focused to shorter timeframes, and our For-You Pages curated to display information that we are interested in. Platforms like TikTok allow Gen-Z to create our own content, on our own medium. But at the same time sometimes technology knows me better than I know myself. And this is only the beginning.

In other words, Gen-Z prefers everything in short: short summaries of information (hello SparkNotes), short videos, texting, short articles, etc. These habits make it harder for Gen-Z to focus for longer periods of time, and result in us being more impatient in general. This also manifests into the trend cycle and culture, where trends don't last for too long because Gen-Z gets bored too quickly. Companies need to feed this instant gratification and cater strategy and new products around the fast pace of Gen-Z, because otherwise, Gen-Z will move on to the next thing.

Imposter syndrome

Due to Gen-Z's high use of social media, we are constantly exposed to the accomplishments and best moments of others, which are often not a realistic portrayal of their daily lives. However, there is a pressure to live up to the standards that we strive for, and the things that we do on a daily basis seem inadequate. Although there have been efforts to post more often, to not care about analytics, and to embody one's real life on social media, several posts and content online are still staged, and social media definitely cannot ever paint the real picture of what is going on in a particular person's life.

In my opinion, social media platforms like Instagram are a curated gallery of your life's best moments. But that's exactly the problem; they're your best moments, and not a representation of real life and daily life.

With people constantly comparing themselves to others, this leads to self-esteem issues and can even lead to higher rates of indecisiveness. This also contributes to depression, and according to a study in the Journal of Abnormal Psychology, rates of depression among kids ages fourteen to seventeen increased more than 60 percent. Jean Twenge, who is an expert in the psychology of Gen-Z, a professor of psychology at San Diego State University, and the author of *iGen,* says that "there is an overwhelming amount of data from many different sources, and it all points in the same direction: more mental health issues among American young people."[32]

Think about imposter syndrome like this. Everyone is a brand, and a unique one. But people wish and try to be like other "brands," which is where the problem arises.

The imposter syndrome that Gen-Z faces makes our generation feel like there is always something left to do, some

---

32   Markham Heid, "Depression and Suicide Rates Are Rising Sharply in Young Americans, New Report Says. This May Be One Reason Why," *Time,* March 14, 2019.

next level to achieve. And although this can be beneficial in terms of pushing yourself and wanting to be the best version of yourself, some people can't sleep, or are in a state of perpetual stress and anxiety because of this societal expectation, as well as expectations that individuals put on themselves. A lack of sleep is bad for teens who ideally need eight to ten hours of sleep every night in order for optimal brain development.[33]

With an over-immersion of tech, teens prioritize time with their devices over other important components of their life like sleep, school, or sports. Personally, this has been something that I've experienced as well. Junior year of high school, I would get about two to three hours of sleep every night, commute to New York City at points in the year for my work with the Working Group on Girls, have crew practice, participate in clubs at school, all while taking the hardest set of classes at my high school.

Now this isn't meant to brag by any means possible because put simply, my junior year was nothing short of a trip to hell, and I can't even say it was worth it. I was far from healthy, didn't hang out with any friends, and was always extremely unhappy and stressed. But this is the result of the imposter syndrome I felt. I always needed to do everything and anything to prove myself to the world. Whether that be taking way too many hard classes I didn't end up doing that well in, or not balancing out my extracurriculars.

---

33   Centers for Disease Control and Prevention, "Sleep in Middle and High School Students," accessed February 26, 2021.

This imposter syndrome pressures Gen-Z to form their own authentic, individual brands, where there is a need to be unique and stand out in comparison to others. This contributes to the rise of particular aesthetics that social media feeds and individuals try to embody, as well as unique, niche applications like Depop, Pinterest, and TikTok, where individuals can find specific pieces of clothing, furniture, etc., that fit to their personal brand.

However, this continuous searching can be stressful, and some people can carry out a particular aesthetic better, further ensuing this cycle of imposter syndrome. Several members of Gen-Z also turn to psychedelics as a result of this constant pressure in hopes of creating and entering an alternate reality where no societal constructs hold them back. This can also go the other way, with members of Gen-Z, even some of my own friends, taking drugs like Adderall in order to stay more attentive, and to create more hours in their day to accomplish the things they need to get done, despite this being detrimental to their health.

Imposter syndrome can also manifest as FOMO, which stands for the fear of missing out. Because everyone is always doing something online, it's hard to keep up, and there's always a sense of not doing enough, or missing out if you're not online. I know this has found its way into my own life, from begging my parents to drive me to the new coffee shop on the street that everyone can't get enough of or longing to go on vacations my family couldn't go on. Gen-Zers need to give the intention of momentum in our increasingly competitive and capitalistic society.

Cancel Culture

People are growing constantly. Kids are getting online profiles younger, and these very children are easily influenced by their parent's or family's thinking. Not being able to formulate their own opinions, and then putting everything online is harmful, and what plants the seeds for someone being cancelled.

What is being cancelled exactly? According to Merriam Webster, it means to "stop giving support" to a particular person, usually a celebrity or influencer.[34] However, this can happen to anyone, anywhere. And what sucks about the internet is that nothing ever gets erased, even a search in a search engine. This is why being cancelled is something that any internet user tries to avoid. Sometimes however, being cancelled is inevitable, because people truly don't know any better.

Jonah Bromwich of the *New York Times* wrote, "Everyone Is Canceled." The clever online version of the article even has a fun illustration where you can enter any word, press search, and a pop up will appear stating your input is cancelled. This article, which I encourage everyone to check out, goes into the nuances of what being cancelled is and the different levels of being cancelled.[35] With the risk of being cancelled so prevalent, sometimes people are afraid to be their authentic selves and are hyperaware of everything that they put on the internet (which can be both a good and bad thing). Even people who haven't done something necessarily bad can be deemed cancelled, seemingly on a whim.

34 *Merriam-Webster.* s.v. "canceled," Accessed Feb 26, 2021.
35 Jonah Engel Bromwich, "Everyone is Canceled," *The New York Times*, June 28, 2018.

Blurred line between work and home

Growing up online has presented Gen-Z with a particular predicament not faced by prior generations—an increasingly thin line between work and home. As stated by Lesley Jane Seymour, who I talk to later in the book: "creativity comes out of the relaxed mind, it does not come out of a mind that is constantly working." Working Gen-Zers in the current age are almost running like sweatshops, working more than forty hours a week. That includes taking calls on weekends, personal days, and having little to no boundaries within a particular job because everyone is available twenty-four-seven.

Prior to the internet, and prior to the cellphone, you went to work, clocked in your hours, and went home after a workweek to a weekend where you couldn't be easily disturbed. However, this isn't the case anymore. Gen-Zers are constantly attached to their job, as they can be contacted anytime. Maintaining and setting boundaries where one cannot be reached or will not take work calls is what Gen-Z struggles with and needs to define in the future.

It's almost as if we need to develop new workweek (for example a four-day week or thirty-hour weeks instead of forty) in order to stay sane, and to make change and move our world forward. These boundaries, in addition to rising cases in poorer mental health, anxiety, and the overwhelming nature of social media can sometimes lead to social media being the potential downfall of our generation. We need to continually ask ourselves: how much is too much?

Lack of soft, social skills

Gen-Z is online. Probably more than they are interacting with people in person, in real life. Everything is online, and it's almost as if there is nothing left to do without a particular device. With the majority of Gen-Z's days being spent online, it makes it harder to develop softer skills that past generations have acquired in terms of communication, emotional intelligence, and growth.

Seven soft skills that you need to achieve career growth according to *HubSpot* blog are:
- Emotional Intelligence; often referred to as the ability to recognize and manage your emotions and the emotions of others.
- Team Player Attitude
- Growth Mindset
- Openness to Feedback
- Adaptability
- Active Listening, Work Ethic[36]

Although Gen-Z has these skills to an extent, we are not experts in such areas, and the lack of these skills leads to mishandlings of situations, a lack of communication, low adaptability in unchangeable situations, and more. Without these key social skills, there are unavoidable workplace situations that can amplify a small misunderstanding into a much larger issue. This is something that other generations have that are extremely beneficial for Gen-Z to learn and to provide an edge in the increasingly hard skilled filled job market of Gen-Z.

---

36 Sophia Bernazzani, "7 Soft Skills You Need to Achieve Career Growth," *HubSpot Blog*, November 16, 2017.

Multitasking and burnout

With everything that is going on, Gen-Z is doing several things at one time. Can't miss the next episode of your favorite show, but have a paper due tonight? Why not do both? Gen-Z has found ways to do a lot of things at once, and although this can work for many, it can sometimes lead to lower quality work, and a lower efficiency in general.

Instead of taking an hour to complete that paper with 100 percent focus, and then getting the rest of the night to watch that show, oftentimes, Gen-Z is doing both, and in comparison, it might take three hours to get through the paper while watching the show, and that three-hour block would result in an average paper, and not a full understanding of what went down during the show.

Gen-Z often has so many small tasks that get put off and never done—a thousand tabs on their browsers—and this results in burnout, because there is just so much to get done and little skill in focusing. Although the work that our generation completes is astounding, we could be more effective if there was less focusing on how to do more, and more focus on how to complete the tasks.

Mental health issues

With everything that Gen-Z has to process, there is no question that mental health is an issue for our generation. Later in the book, I will share discussions I had with some people regarding the collective trauma that Gen-Z already carries. In addition, the sheer pressures from society play a big role in mental health. More education and awareness around the issue of mental health has made people realize that they may have potentially overlooked their own mental health issues.

In addition to more resources, there are also more conversations happening around mental health, along with a general de-stigmatization of the topic as Gen-Z moves into the future. Things like "mental health days" are starting to become more common, and mental health is starting to be seen as a parallel to physical health conditions, as it should.

Mental health is complex and has a lot of factors that differ by individual, but in general, the factors that affect Gen-Z are social media, education, building their own personal brand, maintaining authenticity in their actions, the current state of the world, doing their part to contribute to social good, expectations from society and family, and their ultimate success and path in the future.

Lack of authenticity

Gen-Z thrives on authenticity, but this is often the most difficult part of their online lives. Gen-Zers are often living double lives, having different personas in person and in real life compared to how they portray themselves online. These double lives and personas can blur lines for people between who they actually are, and who they are trying to be or portray online.

An introverted person might have over fifty thousand followers online. Such altering personas make things complicated, contributing to mental health issues and the constant dread of not living up to particular expectations for your online or in-person persona. Online, you can be almost anyone, with filters, presets, and apps to change your body structure, smooth skin, remove fat, remove acne, and put makeup on an otherwise bare face. There really is no limit to what you can do online, and sometimes people look completely different in person compared to their perfect, edited, pristine pictures on their Instagram feed. This is the problem with interactions online because they are always perfected to the desired image of the creator, and this grants the creator a level of control that simply isn't possible in real life.

Why Gen-Zers won't be giving our kids iPads and iPhones early on

People in the tech industry don't give their kids social media; all of their children's devices need to be out of the bedroom, no social media until high school, and they work out a time budget on how much devices can be used.[37] Right now, this might seem cruel, but Gen-Zers are headed down a similar path when it comes to what we'll give our kids. On TikTok, several creators have expressed desires to not give their children iPads, in the hopes that their children won't be consumed with social media and being online at a young age, and for our children to actually have a social life interacting with others.

By the time that Gen-Zers are parents, the world will have changed drastically. A lot of Gen-Zers might not become parents at all or have only one or two children per household as compared to larger households of generations past. Gen-Z's children are going to be brought up differently because we've seen firsthand what the internet can do to a young person. We can understand the nuances of internet life whereas

---

37   *The Social Dilemma*, Netflix.

Gen-Z's parents right now have a disconnect between their children in terms of understanding social media expectations, Gen-Z slang, and the multiple facets that are associated with being online.

Gen-Zers will want their children to know who they are and have a good sense of who they want to be before getting online and being influenced by other people. We will want our kids to use social media and the internet as a platform for growth, and we will know how to navigate and introduce such a revolutionary tool to our children, step by step.

The movie: *The Social Dilemma*

This Netflix original went viral. Ironic.

One of the best lines of the movie? "We've turned into an age of information to disinformation," said by Tristan Harris, a former Google design ethicist, and co-founder and president of The Center for Humane Technology. Harris continued into a great example, stating that around fifty white guys that are twenty to thirty-five years old are making decisions that impact billions of people.

"People will have thoughts that they didn't intend to have because a designer at Google said this is how notifications work on the screen that we wake up to in the morning."
—TRISTAN HARRIS

This goes to show the limited ethics behind the internet and technology.

This movie, released in September of 2020, was months into the world's quarantine. Within this period of time, everyone was "overdue for a digital detox," and Gen-Z recognized this with many doing "Zoom school" as well. We recognized that our mental health and constant, almost mindless, scrolling was an issue. Something had to be done.

This movie rocked social media. People all over the world were talking about the film. It brought attention to data privacy and how much social media and social platforms are changing the way that we think.

Now I want to address privacy for a quick second. Gen-Z doesn't really understand privacy because we've never had it. From the day we were born or from our childhood, our parents posted pictures of us on their new Facebook accounts. There's some probably some embarrassing childhood pictures of almost every Gen-Zer out there because we've been online since day one, and anything that is posted on the internet doesn't go away (even after you delete it).

I personally don't mind clicking the "yes" button whenever websites say that they want me to accept cookies (cookies help websites keep track of your visits and activity) or when sites want me to link my personal Google account to the site granting access to my information.[38]

A good section of the film also included examples in which the tech industry was more powerful than governments and had the tools available to shape society. But the existential

---

38   "What are cookies?" *Norton LifeLock,* August 12, 2019.

question that the movie truly posed was: what are we going to do about it? Tech and social media can't be changed on an individual level, so how can we, as a society, move toward a better future that is more ethical with technology?

So, let's take a deep dive. Here's what I got from the movie, and things you should keep in mind. Social media is in the business of selling their users. Because users don't pay for the products we use, advertisers pay for the products that we use. So essentially, advertisers are the customers, the ones that are actually giving money to the tech companies. Users are the product, and the media is competing for our attention.

The business model of social platforms is to keep you engaged on the screen, figure out how to get your attention, and understand how much of your life you can give to the company, and how they can increase it. As said by Jaron Lanier, computer scientist and founding father of virtual reality, in the film, "It's the gradual, slight, imperceptible change in your own behavior and perception that is the product."[39]

Let that line sink in. Re-read it; "*It's the gradual, slight, imperceptible change in your own behavior and perception that is the product.*"

Social media basically advertises that with a set amount of money, this network can change the world 1 percent in the direction you want it to change; and that's a guarantee. A guarantee that is irresistible to advertisers where social media networks can sell certainty.

---

39   Ibid.

But for that to work, "you have to have great produc-
tions, and for that you need a lot of data."
—SHOSHANA ZUBOFF, PROFESSOR EMERITUS AT
HARVARD BUSINESS SCHOOL; AUTHOR OF "THE
AGE OF SURVEILLANCE CAPITALISM."

Online, everything that you do is being tracked and measured, down to images and how long you look at an image.
This feeds information into an algorithm, or models, with
little to no human supervision that are getting better and
better predictions about what we're going to do and who
we are. The algorithm knows when its users are lonely, or
depressed, and then adjusts the content that is shown on
their feed accordingly.

So essentially, it's not the data that is being sold, but rather
what is being done with the data. There are several social
media platforms, and whoever has the best model wins.

One thing to keep in mind about algorithms is that they're
not objective, they're subjective. Algorithms can be seen as
opinions embedded in code and are optimized to some definition of success. An example of algorithms can be seen with
three simple words. Type in "climate change is..." into Google.
Depending on where you live, the suggested fourth word to
complete that search will be different. In a more liberal state,
the search could suggest "real" or "a big problem," whereas
in a more conservative state, the search could yield "fake
news" or "not real."

The unfortunate truth about algorithms is that they provide users with a false sense that everyone agrees with you because everyone that is in your news feed thinks and agrees with you, creating an echo chamber of your own views. According to an internal Facebook report in 2018, 64 percent of the people who joined extremist groups on Facebook did so because the algorithms steered them there. "Algorithms promote content that sparks outrage, hate, and amplifies biases within the data that we feed them."[40]

Engagement, growth, and advertising are the three goals being optimized by algorithms.

Engaging the audience and the user on the application, growing the number of users on the application, and getting more advertisers to generate even more revenue are the goals of algorithms. But how can technical tech achieve these more "humane" goals? The answer is persuasive tech.

Such design is implemented to an extreme level where the goal is to modify a person's behavior to the extent of them making a decision that they normally wouldn't have made. This is all possible through positive intermittent reinforcement. And this is what drives AI, or artificial intelligence. AI elicits responses from users, and repeatedly hits the human brain with dopamine, a neurotransmitter that makes humans feel pleasure, or just feel good. Since humans are social creatures and feel good with social interaction, social media presents an overload of dopamine, leading to addiction.[41]

---

40   Ibid.
41   Ibid.

In a few words, social media uses your own psychology against yourself.

"They're so conditioned that they practically can't help behaving as they ought to behave"

—ALDOUS HUXLEY, *BRAVE NEW WORLD*, 1932

Now, how has Gen-Z been impacted?

Online connection has become primary, especially for new generations like Gen-Z. Even seemingly harmless connections on social media are being handled by a sneaky third person financing it—paying to manipulate these two people into connecting. Gen-Zers are being raised in a context where the meaning of culture and communication is manipulation, and deceit is at the center of everything we do. As we downloaded social media early, social media has taken over our sense of self-worth and identity. We tie our self-worth around the number of followers, likes, comments, and shares we get, which is arbitrary. These networks weren't designed by child psychologists that wanted to nurture children, but rather tech giants looking for optimal profit.

A five-thousand-person study found that higher social media use correlated with self-reported decline in mental and physical health and life satisfaction according to the American Journal of Epidemiology in 2017. "Persuasive technology design like an endless feed to scroll through or push notifications create a feedback loop that keep up glued to our devices. Notifications work to get our attention, and that's what's so dangerous about them. As said by Aldous Huxley in 1958, "They failed to take into account man's infinite appetite for distractions."[42]

We have, over time, evolved to think about what a couple of people in our community may think about us. However, we are not evolved to think about what ten thousand-plus people think of us, or about social approval being dosed to us every five minutes on our devices. But, Gen-Z has to grow up with this.

If something is a tool, it is just sitting there. If something is not a tool, it has demands, and it is manipulating you to do something. That's what social media is.

So what can you do about this? It's simple: work to outsmart the algorithm.

Here are some tips to do just that.

- Turn off your notifications. Stop letting the algorithm drag you back in and give you a reason to check your device. Make your online time that you set aside and intentionally want to spend.
- Set screen time goals and stick to them.
- Use browsers like Qwant, instead of Google, that will help reduce algorithmic effects on your browsing. There are also countless extensions on Chrome and other browsers that can remove browser recommendations for you.[43]

---

42 Ibid.
43 Ibid.

- Try to steer away from accepting videos or content recommended to you. This will only feed into the algorithm and make it easier to get to know you and your likings.
- Have conversations and create a space for it. Follow people that are on the complete opposite of your views and beliefs, so your feed and browsing isn't an echo chamber of your own ideas. Make a conscious effort to go out of your "For-You" page.
- Realize that *you vote with your clicks.* You create financial incentive for those who are making profit based on your viewing and interests online. Be mindful and aware of that when you are online.

We can change what social media looks like and what it means; social media isn't set into stone, it can be changed, and changed for the better. We built social media, and we have a responsibility to change it. We need to have conversations about the whole story, not just what is displayed on social media, to stop polarization amplified by such social networks.

This conversation can even extend into changes in policy in the future. As we are starting to see, laws that are designed for an analog world aren't fit for a digital world.

This chapter is a big caveat to the overall tech-positive nature of this book. Although tech has its downsides, it has changed the world, and started to level the playing field for a lot of people. There is always change to be made, but using tech as a resource is something that Gen-Z can harness for greater social good. Gen-Z also has grown up with the internet, so we have a more innate ability to detect when something is right or wrong on the internet, including scams and traps. Our generation is the one that will demand tech to change for the better, for ourselves and for future generations.[44]

44 Ibid.

Chapter 6

Access to resources

———

Gen-Z has access to the internet, and the internet is a magical place. For forty-nine dollars on Coursera, you can get a certificate from an Ivy League university. Top companies like Google, Apple, and Microsoft offer free courses online that one can take at any time. In terms of education, Codeacademy and Khan Academy are revolutionizing the education space, and of course, you have the handy search engine, where you type an answer, and you receive one in less than a second. When one says that Gen-Z has access to resources, this is no understatement.

Education is something that is really defining who we are as a generation, and our ability to learn and process information differently and through various mediums than other generations is what sets us apart. In this chapter, I'll be talking to Katie Tracy, a YouTuber and international student who makes content on education, Julia Terpak, who educates others about Gen-Z on TikTok, and Ali Sait, a campaign staffer in Texas, whose team is shifting campaign strategies to focus on the time that people spend online versus the hit-or-miss signs and information they might see in person.

Creation tools are more than prevalent, as there are new ways and mediums in which to create content and spread information online through social platforms and the internet. Gen-Z knows how to use these very creation tools to **create compelling digital content for little to no cost.** Advertising has taken on a whole new form, with Google and Facebook ads more effective than television, print, or billboard ads by exponential margins.

Capitalizing on the time people spend on their devices and making sure particular companies or interests can make the best of that time is a key strategy for moving forward.

Ali Sait

Talking about Ali Sait, I can only think of the radiating passion he exudes about his work. Sait is currently directing communications for a congressional race in Austin, Texas, working to flip the currently Republican district to a Democratic one through innovations in one of American's fundamental rights: voting. Sait is working on a campaign that has been endorsed by all the political celebrities, like Bernie Sanders and Elizabeth Warren, all while becoming a freshman at the University of Chicago. Ali's sheer experience at such a young age really goes to show the capacity and potential of Gen-Z. Ali's willingness to contribute to this campaign shows how we are invested and interested in change. Ali's role in the campaign displays how Gen-Z makes our own opportunities and are good at them.

My conversation with Ali started around four words: a lack of change. These four words define the political cycle, where "every two years you have an election cycle and the same issues are discussed in the same ways without progress being made on any front," which then leads to "polarizing conditions" that result in extremes within the political system. These extremes then start news cycles, and headlines from these news cycles fall into the hands of readers, who then are fed this information every day.

Sait mentioned that after facing a particular issue for a set number of years, the solutions for this particular issue start to become more extreme, and every couple of years, something new and radical will come up. He said that "while more progressive politics is a good thing, I think that there is a risk of going too far, where in just a two-year term you can expect the world to change. And then the polarizing conditions will basically prevent that from happening in the first place, when in fact you're contributing to that polarization by expecting more in a shorter period of time."

Although not publicized, in many ways Gen-Z is more conservative than we might be perceived to be, and especially fiscally. We've grown up around instability, whether it be the 2008 financial crisis, or even the global coronavirus pandemic. We want to be secure, but we also want to make sure that people are being treated fairly and equally. We've seen the bad and want to make sure that we are prepared for any circumstance that we are put under in the future. This places Gen-Z at an intersection of conservatism and liberalism that we are trying to figure out.

According to *Business Insider*, "Instagram and social media play a big role in how Gen-Z gets their political news."[45] Why does this make a difference? One, because representatives can capitalize on the time that their constituents spend on social media and use ads and their own social media accounts to influence the opinions of Gen-Zers. Second, being online creates an echo chamber of ideas. Representatives now have to figure out how to navigate the online space in order to gain the support of their constituents and new constituents since echo chambers make it difficult to break into new spaces. This makes being an advocate for constituents harder as well, especially Gen-Zers who are ready to call officials out on any action.

According to a poll done by *Business Insider*, there is common sentiment, especially in the United States among Gen-Zers, that the current state of the country is going very "poorly," with 36 percent of Gen-Z answering poorly, and 19 percent answering very poorly.[46] What does this statistic show? It shows how much Gen-Z desires change and wants to see that change via their elected representatives.

Our generation has so many issues to worry about, and Ali's point comes into play here. *Within the last decade of politics, yes, changes have been made, but to what extent?* The rhetoric that a majority of Gen-Z presents is that it is up to our generation to solve many of the world's crises, like climate change, racial injustice, and gun control. Even though these

---

45 Kate Taylor, "Instagram is Gen Z's go-to source of political news—and it's already having an impact on the 2020 election," *Business Insider*, July 1, 2019.

46 Ibid.

are rampant issues that are affecting our country, the efforts of Gen-Z need to be supplemented with action from those in power, at least until we are able to get into such positions.

Here's an example to explain what I mean: Gen-Z led a series of climate change protests in 2019, showing Gen-Z's concern about climate change and desire for change, with the US's plan to pull out of the Paris Climate Agreement. This shows that Gen-Z cares and other generations do too, enough so that they followed Gen-Z's lead. Therefore, Gen-Z is in a position where they are "politically homeless," and not able to do much, at least until we are the ones in positions of power in the future.

With the knowledge that is readily available to Gen-Z at their fingertips, they are able to educate themselves on things like the United States' flawed electoral system, where being a youth is adversity enough, but being a minority or a person of color places one in even more of a disposition in the current system. This drives the demands of Gen-Z up, but without much way of solutions. Another point that is highlighted in even AP United States history (Advanced Placement US History is a high school class also known as APUSH) is our termed presidency. Presidents always play it safe and get little work done in their first term in order to secure a nomination for another term and establish their credibility and effectiveness in the Oval Office. So essentially, don't do anything crazy, and you might get another four years in the office.

Ali commented on this system, and even brought it in terms of the 2020 election for the presidency with Joe Biden, saying that Biden's first terms "will not actually be focused on moving forward but rather repairing all the damage, which is then problematic for the midterms in 2022." And this brings us back to the cycle of "no change;" again, there is this expectation of change when in reality they're just basically fixing everything that was broken and trying to move forward. After this is accomplished, then one can actually start to work on progressive reform.

When I asked Ali about the notion of Cloutivism (the act of doing things just to do things, and taking performative actions) he said, "that's kind of the problem." We have lots of people posting content relevant to activism and what is going on in today's world, and then you have people dedicating their lives to creating change. The sad part is that you won't really know the difference between those two individuals based on what you're seeing on their social media. This idea of "fake activism," and this facade that people put up online, by reposting stories and content, "is fine, as long as the fake activism creates a need for someone to do something deeper."

Content on social media (if read) serves two goals, and those goals are education and awareness. These posts provide the opportunity for one to be able to step out of their shoes into those of another individual that might be suffering due to a particular social issue that is affecting them. With reshares of posts, and the circulation of such information, awareness about a particular issue can be raised.

However, what social media lacks is actual change, which adds to Sait's earlier point. But, if someone is posting a lot of information on a particular topic on social media to the point where they think, "oh, maybe I should get more involved," that's the important step in all of this because it doesn't matter how you get involved, but at least now, you're in a place where you can help make change. Sait emphasized the importance of this key transition between social media activism, into physical action like voting and volunteering.

Ali Sait. Let's circle back. What makes Ali's work special? Facebook and social media ads. Ali and his fellow team of Gen-Zers ran several types of social media ads. What does running ads mean? Essentially, any organization, individual, or company can pay social media networks to place strategic ads in order for people to see their product, message, or service listed as an advertisement as they scroll on social media. Political campaigns, at least the more modern ones, are steering away from expensive expenditures like television ads, which can cost millions of dollars in total (a large sum of a budget) and instead are investing such money into social media ads, which will strategically reach more people and guarantee a particular effect. (Refer back to yup...tech has its downsides.)

Ali and his team run a couple of different types of ads:

- Facebook ads that target people who may be involved in social media activism, to get more people in their community to vote, and to engage around a particular candidate.
- Target kids on social media that might convey voting information to their parents who can actually vote.
- Running targeted voter registration ads and partnering with companies where instead of donating to the campaign, you can donate two dollars to register a Democratic voter in their district. Using AI, Ali's team have

basically found all the unregistered Democrats in the district. With this incentive, people are more likely to sign up to vote, and get the candidate in office.

So, what does all this mean? Our generation genuinely wants to make change. Although it's a common thread that runs within our generation, there are enough Gen-Zers who are committed to their work, and enough Gen-Zers willing to think outside the box in order to come up with innovative solutions that will impact their communities.

Katie Tracy

In Katie Tracy's words, *"Being a student has always been a very big part of my life because it changed a lot of my perspective."* Katie is a current student at Cornell, and being an international student, having attended international school when she was in the Philippines, was the first time she was exposed to a very different set of values. What kept her grounded however was her access to resources and different social media networks to find her space as a creative.

First on Tumblr as a blogger, Katie expanded on her interests in coding and UI/UX design by exploring social media sites like Tumblr, which reached peak popularity in 2011. From there, Katie's growth on social media evolved from Tumblr, to Instagram, and then to YouTube.

Katie describes her YouTube channel as a "reflection of things that are going on in my life, that (she) wants to document." Through her experiences at Cornell and as a high-achieving student, Katie is able to put herself out there. She says that the algorithms most of the time work in your favor as they connect you with people who are also interested in your content and what you are putting out there.

So, why is matching with someone on the algorithm important? Two words: representation and relatability. This is one reason why TikTok is doing so well: because the algorithm is able to match people with others who would like their content, extremely well in fact. Finding representation of a particular concept, of a particular perspective, like Katie's, being an international student at an Ivy League, to being able to relate to a content creator on any platform, is what drives up interaction on social media and helps creators easily find their niche.

Other tools to be successful on social media are marketing tools, SEO, and strategy. Such ploys could be using particular hashtags, filters, SEO (search engine optimization), which improves the quality and quantity of web traffic to a web page from different search engines, and to use trending effects on the internet in order for people to find content more easily on social platform-based algorithms. Such account strategy can even be homing in on a particular niche more and analyzing one's audience base in order to optimize content to raise engagement.

Such resources allow Katie and other creators to be successful and find people who are ready to engage in the content that they put out. And Katie is able to tap into an audience that is processing information about education differently, and through different forms of media, like YouTube.

Julia Terpak

Julia Terpak is the founder of Gen Z Connect, a platform made to create meaningful discussions about the unique advantages and disadvantages of our generation.

To Julia, the hardest part about being a content creator is consistency, especially while working a full-time job simultaneously. "People like to downplay what goes into creating content, but it's a lot of pressure to stay on top of creating high-quality, entertaining content. You rarely feel relaxed as a small content creator and feel that if you slack off just one day your reach will become stagnant or nonexistent."

Julia is a Gen-Zer herself, and she has been creating content since the age of twelve when she would edit YouTube videos. Almost a decade later, this passion led her to create Gen Z Connect, which is on TikTok and Instagram and has a podcast. Through this platform, Julia aims to empower the youth to create a better future. We are so lucky to be living in such advanced times, and we need to utilize our strengths, accessibility, and knowledge to better the human experience. Julia said that when she first got into the space, she was only seeing conversations about the Millennial generation. She wanted to create a narrative about Gen-Z in order to inform and motivate.

Julia talked about how trial and error were key. She said that "You have to get out of your comfort zone to find out what you love." For Julia, her passions are content creation and starting discussions about the future. Julia said how she would find herself watching YouTube videos on topics like technology and innovation for hours.

When it came to content creation, it came naturally to some extent, but then a lot of work had to go into it on the other hand. Julia said that the hard part of content creation is putting yourself out there, being able to handle criticism. "You have to really know yourself, your intent, and be mentally strong enough to handle the subliminal pressures that come with it. That was very out of my comfort zone at first, and I had to really challenge myself and get out of my comfort zone to figure out if I could continue with my passion for content creation."

When I asked Julia what she thought makes content or posts get a lot of views and likes, she said that "Your content has to tell a story in some sense. From beginning, middle, to end, there has to be something that makes viewers/users wanting more. 'More' could be going to your account to see more pictures/videos, watching a video multiple times, loving or hating a post enough to feel the need to comment, wanting to share the post with others, etc. All of these factors play into the social media algorithms and in return, increase your exposure."

Gen-Z uses social media very authentically, as it has become ingrained in every aspect of our lives. Our generation doesn't look at it so much as a separate entity, but more so just a part of our daily lives.

Gen-Z has a large age range, so Julia focuses on making her content more lighthearted, even if she's touching on a serious topic. On TikTok for example, Julia's dances interest the eight-year-olds, but the important topics she's speaking about interest the older ages of Gen-Z. Keeping her content easily digestible, aesthetically pleasing, and short keeps Gen-Z's attention, as our average attention span is only eight seconds and we crave instant gratification. So, this approach works well.[47]

When I talked to Julia about success on social media, she told me that "a successful social media account to me has nothing to do with numbers. Effort, quality, and intent is everything. If what you are doing represents hard work and wanting to leave a positive impact, you're successful." She continued to talk about measuring success, and how it's easy to let numbers build you up or tear you down. However, Terpak said that if she doesn't feel authentic about what she's posting, she feels unsuccessful. "Even if a video is doing well, if I don't fully align with the intent anymore, I will take it down. I measure my success on social media by how prideful I feel about what I'm putting out into the world."

We've grown up with the world at our fingertips. We've been exposed to people around the country and world from a young age; aka, we've been exposed to different races, ethnicities, and cultures from a young age. Inclusivity is expected and just a part of the way we were brought up. Other generations did not have the access to the world that we have growing up with the internet, and they were confined to the demographics of their towns, cities, and social circles.

When I asked Julia how she deals with any negativity or controversy, she said that she sets her intentions and as long as she knows they're pure, she can sleep at night. People will

---

47   Thomas J Law, "10 Vital Strategies to use When Marketing to Gen-Z," *Oberlo*, November 3, 2020.

always have something to say. People will always find a way to misunderstand you or take things out of context. I make sure to be open-minded to criticism because I'm not perfect and can certainly do wrong, but I have to keep human nature and the current internet climate in mind to an extent. People choose their perception!

In ten or twenty years, Julia said that Gen-Z will continue to intertwine with technology as this is an inevitable aspect of our future. We will continue utilizing that to our advantage to hopefully create a better human experience. Whether that's utilizing the advantages of technology to be able to create a quicker and less expensive college experience, or even a better work-life balance.

When I asked Julia about her advice to Gen-Z, she said that

"Self-awareness is everything. We are not 'better' than any other generation, but we have the tools and ability to do more good than has been done by any other generation in the past. We have to be aware of our weaknesses and tackle them head-on to create change within ourselves. Once we do that, we can begin to create even more positive change within the world."

Chapter 7

Networking, and forming connections

With the internet, social media, and websites where we can interact with one another, our network is expanding, both personally and professionally. One might go to a virtual event on a topic that one is interested in and meet people from across the world at the event, and then develop a relationship. Such relationships and informal networking are growing our networks beyond traditional networking, where one has to go to events, or connect with people strategically. Networking in today's world is as easy as sending a cold message on LinkedIn, Instagram, or tagging someone on Twitter. You can also find people that are more aligned to your particular views and interests easier through online groups and communities.

In our world today, out network is almost as valuable as our skillsets. And you might be saying, not everyone has a network! My answer is, build one.

Thousands of high schoolers have joined the LinkedIn space, formerly only for professionals (I'd argue that some high schoolers are professionals, but I digress). This has not only allowed students and Gen-Zers access to a professional network at a young age but has also opened up doors to connect to other highly motivated high school students. Knowing what is necessary in the workspace to succeed allows high schoolers to gain the skills they need in order to become executives earlier.

Growing our network is of utmost importance in the future. Not only does it provide usefulness in terms of getting information or perspectives other than our own, but it also provides usefulness in staying on top of trends and brainstorming new ideas for the next big thing.

I got to talk to Anna Blue on the importance of network. (More about Anna in **Collective trauma, and bridging generations.**) Talking to Anna, the one thing that she emphasized was the importance of network. She told me that "at least in corporate America, it's very much about who you know, and the relationships that you build. But, at the same time we second guess ourselves, and Gen-Z does this a lot."

She says that she encourages young people to think about who's in your network, think about the network that you're creating, and the network that you want to have. We are all living in a virtual world, and although you might not be networking in person, "you have access to every CEO in the world on LinkedIn. From there, it's about formulating." Anna says that she personally responds to every young person that reaches out to her. In terms of networking, Anna advises

Gen-Zers to capitalize on the fact that you're young, as there's a big difference between a forty-two-year-old reaching out to a CEO. They're going to look at what value the forty-two-year-old brings to them, and if that forty-two-year-old is worth their time.

When you reach out to high-level people as a young person, and use your age, express what you hope to learn from the individual and ask if they could give you ten to fifteen minutes of their time. In just fifteen minutes, you can establish a relationship. Just reach out to people and say, "I'm young, and I want to be where you are someday. Do you have time for three questions? Do you have the ten minutes to spare?"

Several people end up second guessing themselves, saying that "this person isn't going to want to talk to me," and questioning what you have. What you do have is your own power, your own value that is really important to people, especially when you're talking about brands, who want to build a relationship with you, which is equally valuable for them. Collaborating with brands is something that Gen-Z is extremely used to and is in the perfect niche to complete.

Brands want to know: as a consumer, what do you like, and what don't you like? This can be a mutually beneficial relationship, and all you need is the confidence to start out. As Anna says, "No, is the worst you're going to get. They're not going to show up at your house, and they're not going to hurt you." And of course, some people won't respond, and you can always chalk it up to, "that person didn't have the time or maybe didn't see it," and you move on.

It's mastering the art of the no. It's about being okay with a no and making it a yes. Maybe someone can't jump on a phone call. Message them and ask a question, and they might be able to see your interest through such a question, and your knowledge on the subject.

Additionally, your network is also valuable among your peers. As Anna says, "it's a huge, missed opportunity to not network among your peers. You have no idea who any of you will be. One of your high school friends could get declared for the NBA Draft, or be a CEO, but you didn't know that when you all were sixteen. You never know who anyone is going to be in your circle. Continue to be mindful of the people you surround yourselves with, even just for your own self-care, for your own mental health. Identify the people that take the best care of you, that help you be you because that's going to make you your best self. You're going to get to be that CEO because you surround yourself with people who see you for exactly who you are, no matter how you show up, in good ways and in bad ways."

LinkedIn—yeah, Gen-Zers are on there

LinkedIn. As of now, it's a very professional space, with not that many high schoolers on there. And I'm possibly writing from a perspective of a high-achieving student. However, Gen-Z wants to grow. Gen-Z wants to evolve, and learn, because we know we don't learn skills like networking, connecting, and job growth at school. Gen-Z has a desire and ability to grow in a professional network as well. As an online platform, LinkedIn gives us, internet natives, more comfortability in adjusting and learning the ins and outs of the platform.

I'll write from experience here. As I'm writing this, I have 3,284 followers on LinkedIn, and I created my profile around nine months ago. When I first downloaded the app, and created my profile, I was lost. I was seeing other high schoolers and college students with amazing profiles, and also, people like my parents, not taking much interest in the site. So, I was really confused; was there value in the site? I started to play around with the site, started to get to know the features, and then started editing my own profile, and building from there.

I really grew my account over the summer, where every day, I would have five to ten networking calls with people from all over the world—whose perspective I wanted to hear, who I wanted to learn from, and about. Now, this was on the high end, and doing all of this comes with privilege. Having the time to put into this, and not having to do anything else during the summer as well is a privilege. But I learned how to network and how to do it well. I even connected with three other high schoolers I started a start-up with. Now, that wasn't a successful venture, but we talked to people from professors to investors about our start-up, and simply connected via LinkedIn.

Now, my friends call me the "networking queen" because I'm the one who's able to do the connecting. A friend can tell me that they're interested in neuroscience, and I'll connect them with someone I talked to or messaged. I can reach out to people with no hesitation because I've broken the stigma of cold-emailing or messaging. LinkedIn has made me grow professionally, but it's the same story for Gen-Zers who want to break into the professional world. And you could be thinking, do people really take Gen-Zers seriously? It's a valid question. The answer: yes and no.

Some people aren't open to Gen-Zers being on the platform, but I'd say there's much more value in us being on there. Gen-Zers are willing to take on internships and unpaid jobs that others aren't. We're willing to put in the time and the effort to expand our skillsets. We're the ones that are assets to your teams. One of my bosses has told me that myself and some of my fellow Gen-Zers that worked at her company were much more efficient and better employees than her Millennial or Gen-X counterparts.

The fact of the matter is that Gen-Zers know how to capitalize on opportunity. And although there aren't too many Gen-Zers on the platform as of now, I can almost guarantee that the numbers are growing every day, and that Gen-Zers will be the primary users of the network sooner than later.

Basis of connection for Gen-Z

There's a new dating app. To some people, using a dating app is weird, out of the ordinary, or just plain bizarre. To us, it can be used as a way to make friends and connect with more people. There are dating apps based off of things other generations couldn't even imagine, like music tastes (Tastebuds) or even an app based on astrological compatibility, like Struck.

Gen-Z craves connection. We want to talk and network with people who "vibe" with us and are there to help us navigate the world that lies ahead. With that said however, Gen-Z heavily prioritizes the relationships that we have with ourselves (or at least tries to) before moving forward with other people. This is relevant because with technology, it's hard to gain a sense of who you are as a person, because a lot of our personality traits can be influenced easily by the internet and what is going on, which also means that we are continually changing and evolving as time moves on. Before letting people into our lives, Gen-Z understands that they need to know who they are in order to properly connect with others. Social media, although designed to connect with other people that you know, can be very isolating and lonely at the same time.

Tech's role in our relationships is ever present, and something that we have to navigate every single day. The fact of the matter is that being on technology and the internet since a young age makes our social skills not even comparable to those of our parent's generations. We feel awkward really easily, and we also don't always know what to say or what to do in a lot of situations. A lot of Gen-Zers have social anxiety, and for good reason. One can *control* everything that is put out on the internet. But, in real life, that doesn't always happen.

Tech continues to shape who we are and who we connect with even through a simple "for-you" page or "recommended" page on social media. But this isn't always a bad thing. Because of the internet, we can connect with people, thousands of miles away—people that we've never met before in person—simply based on shared interests. Three of my closest friends, who know everything about my life, from my favorite food to my Instagram follower count, I've never met before. One lives in Mexico, another in California, and another, closer to me, but in New York. For reference, I live in New Jersey.

Yet, despite all odds, I talk to these very people on a daily basis and share everything with them. Even though I've never even given these people a hug, they're the first people that I turn to, whether it be to check out some selfies I just took, or advice in a tough situation.

This is hard to understand for other generations. My parents are absolutely dumbfounded by the concept. However, we as Gen-Zers use this ability to connect to our advantage. We're starting more businesses, nonprofits, and companies, with people that we've never met before. We're able to find *better* people for such ventures through the internet and form lasting connections that are meaningful for both parties.

Because of this, we are able to create around our interests, because it's not a lonely journey anymore. In my progression as an advocate, no one in my town or area really understood what I was doing. And if they did, people weren't very supportive. But online, I found friends who would always "hype me up" and support me every step of the way. In this sense, the community we form online makes it easier to capitalize on our interests, and actually pursue them. That's why you're able to see more Gen-Z creatives, and young people being financially stable while still venturing out and taking part in traditionally unstable careers.

A sentiment across social media platforms is that Gen-Zers don't want to be working a desk job or necessarily buying into corporate culture. Again, this is not representative of all of Gen-Z, but even if one is inclined to work in such a space, Gen-Z longs for creative and fun outlets outside of work as well. This is why we are more likely to monetize around passions and interests of our own. And this is why the world is more confusing in terms of jobs for Gen-Z than any other generation—because there are literally an infinite number of options that you could do—and be successful doing. And if you don't see what you want to do, you can create it—and still be successful. The job market for Gen-Z has much more options and is going to be changing rapidly with much fewer conventional jobs and more creative and intersectional jobs like never before.

Another thing social media has made evident to Gen-Z? What we're missing. These spaces and communities we have created and facilitated online are great, but being a part of these communities makes one aware of what's lacking. Gen-Zers, being on the internet for so long and definitively knowing that the internet and social media are going to be big parts of their lives in the future, strive to fill the lacks and make these spaces better, equitable, and more inclusive for people to be in.

So back to dating apps. Why'd I bring this up? Well, two things.

One, Gen-Z wants to be social, like any other generation. Our way of seeking it is just different. The internet has broadened our perspective in a way where we understand that our hometown or surroundings aren't the people that we are going to be interacting with forever, and if we don't gel with the people that we're around, we look online to fulfill this craving for social connection. No matter what your interests, you can find some sort of site or application that connects people based on similar interests.

Two, Gen-Z is much more comfortable talking about sexuality than other generations. In August of 2020, the song "WAP" came out. A couple hours after the release of the song, it was trending all over TikTok, with a viral dance to come with it. If you don't know what WAP means, you could look it up. And yes, it's a bit out there, and probably not that appropriate for this book. But, it's worth a mention. It's worth talking about because at least in American education, sex education is lacking. And Gen-Z wants to be comfortable with who they are, in terms of sexual orientation and their own bodies.

Gen-Z is willing to talk about such issues, including sexual wellness, birth control, and more. Why? To break the stigma. To stop hiding behind taboo. To embrace authenticity and to make us all feel more human. Circling back to "WAP," the song not only took down barriers in talking about sexuality and autonomy, but also emphasized the importance of females talking about such topics and owning the space. The song, sung and rapped by Cardi B and Megan Thee Stallion, encouraged Gen-Z to also think about females in spaces that were traditionally dominated by men.

A quick fun fact, rapper Cardi B now has more listeners, followers, and global listening status compared to her husband, rapper Offset. This challenging of the status quo is inherently interesting to Gen-Z, and although my mom's face was beyond astounded when she first heard the song, it was still breaking barriers for me, and other Gen-Zers.

So, a network is important. And today, it's easier than ever to build one. Connor Blakely, who I talk to in the next chapter, started his own Gen-Z marketing company at the age of fifteen with the help of Mark Cuban's business advisor Cameron Herold, and connected with him through sending him a couple emails. I got to interview everyone in this book through networking, reaching out, and putting all qualms aside to "shoot my shot" and see where it takes me. And the best part is, you can too.

Chapter 8

Talentless? More Like Talent Filled

Fashion, styled by Gen-Z.

If you didn't get the joke, Scott Disick, who was formerly in a relationship with Kourtney Kardashian, has a brand named Talentless. With the vast resources that Gen-Z has, we all have our unique talents, so why not use the resources available to expound on them and explore who we want to be?

In this chapter, I'll be exploring the stories of Lucie Zhang, Maria Bobila, Matt Sarafa, Jasmine Cheng, and Kristina Ang. These five individuals are different, yet the same. They are driven and have made success for themselves at an extremely young age and are only going to be growing their brands and businesses as they move into the next steps of their lives. I'll be going through fashion, food, trends, culture, and content creation as I dive into the lives of these five individuals.

Now, let me address something before you get further into this chapter. A lot of people in this chapter are in the fashion industry. I did this for two reasons:

- Fashion is a field that intersects with a lot of other fields and incorporates a lot of different components like business, creativity, and even sustainability.
- I love fashion!

And if you need more evidence as to why fashion is so relevant, "The global revenue in the fashion segment will reach $580 Billion in 2019 and is expected to grow at an average of 12 percent for the next few years. Gen-Z wants **convenience**. They look for **athleisure, normcore, gender neutral,** and **comfortable** items. They also want to **be unique, and they feel socially responsible.** Fast fashion is not so fashionable, albeit there are quite a few exceptions. Gen-Zers like brands that promote a diverse, edgy, and authentic vision. Exclusivity is not so much about status but being unique and defining one's identity. Personalization becomes more important than ever."[48]

"Gen-Zers also see fashion almost as an **investing category.** They sell their clothes to buy new ones also mindful of the environmental impact the fashion industry has. They buy clothes they think can increase in value over time—back to Supreme, for instance. **Social platforms**, like Depop, empower Gen-Zs to be able to '*start a fashion business from their bedroom.*' A report from ThredUp estimates that the total **resale** market will more than double to $51 billion in the next five years, representing 10 percent of the total retail

---

48   Fashion, Statista.

market. **Circular fashion** is the new fashion. Outfit inspiration can come from anywhere and anyone. **Trends are not set by brands, clothes are not just bought from stores, and sustainability is a real thing."**[49]

So, let's dive right into it, with arguably the most renowned name in fashion.

Lucie Zhang

Vogue. One of the most iconic and well-renowned magazines in the world, with covers of high editorial fashion, and celebrities gracing these covers with their personas. But, with all of us going down a more digital road, *Vogue* has had to pivot as well: to social media. Lucie Zhang is the associate director of social media at *Vogue.* She creates content and markets the social media feed of the iconic magazine to keep engagement rates high, and her audience coming back for more. Zhang and her team not only adapt all *Vogue* (print and .com) stories for each social media platform, but also program exclusive content/experiences for their social media audiences.

A platform like *Vogue* sets the trends in fashion and design and is considered to some as the "fashion bible." To keep up with the trends, Zhang and her team are always on the lookout for new stars, emerging trends, and current culture and conversations to inspire their content. Zhang says that "to evaluate where you think culture will evolve to next, you have to look to younger generations, who will be our future

---

49 Cayatena Hurtado, "The Subtle Art of (Not) Understanding Gen Z," *Product Hunt.*

leaders and thought-provokers," which is the expansive and diverse Gen-Z.

As Gen-Z is growing older, starting to take part in societal conversations, and becoming more and more involved in society, Gen-Z has started to develop a distinctive voice of their own on social media, from trends that take over the internet, to indie, smaller trends. This means **"what's cool" is constantly changing**, but "what's cool" also differs person to person. I might think that watching a video about food is interesting, where my friend might love something about music. **Our interests are vast, but they also intersect.**

If you read that last paragraph, there's a lot. But Gen-Z is a lot. And *Vogue* is tasked with figuring out how to capitalize on the voice that Gen-Z has and create content that will cater to this audience. By capitalizing on this voice, and the conversations that are being had in the social media sphere, *Vogue* is able to keep up on the trends of Gen-Z. And that means keeping up with whatever means possible.

One of the "biggest differentiating factors for *Vogue* can be summed up in one word: access." With the *Vogue* name comes the *Vogue* privilege, with access to top talent, behind-the-scenes exclusives, incredible creatives, etc., therefore making the content sometimes come to *Vogue* itself.

Sometimes, it's almost as if something you were texting with your friends about, or a trend on Instagram or TikTok, is written about the next day, and that is how content stays fresh and relevant. But this also has a downside. Zhang said that the hardest part of her job "is probably having to be 'on'

24/7. The Internet doesn't take a night off, vacation or week-end, so our team has adapted to make sure there is coverage and oversight 24/7."

Establishing boundaries between work and home is some-thing that Gen-Z struggles with. Growing up with the internet, Gen-Z hasn't had the experience of being able to put away their phones or laptops for the weekend, but are rather available; wherever, whenever. This contributes to the mental health problem that our generation faces. Because we're online practically 24/7, it's hard to set clear boundaries between work and home, which leads to more anxiety, and possibly mental health problems, a lack of rest, or lack of healthy habits.

But *fashion, beauty, and entertainment trends have always been a reflection of culture, politics, and society today.* So, rather than demographics, I think psychographics are probably what we think in terms of because someone who wants to stay on the cutting edge of culture can exist within any age range.

When I asked Zhang what a successful social media account looks like to her, she responded with "if it elicits an emotional response. Analytically, you can measure it through engage-ment metrics, but I think the intangible feeling of adding something to the conversation that you think is important is also valuable. So, success is telling a story that we feel we are uniquely positioned to tell best, and that other people resonate with as a result."

Despite being a physical manifestation of something, suc-cess in social media can be measured by the emotions that are felt by the audience of a particular account, whether it be "happiness, excitement, joy, sadness, etc." Social media is "meant to be a tool for human connection. The best accounts bring a personality to a page" that really replace or are a substitute for this connection that we all as a human race desire. The fact of the matter is that humans are social animals, and with more of us working at home, and fewer experiences and opportunities to go out and meet new people, social media is becoming the way in which we can fulfill this need for a social connection. *The most successful accounts are those that can empathize with us, that relate to us, and give us that connection that we desire.*

Gen-Z differs in comparison to other generations in their interactions and actions on social media, because

we've been raised in a digital world, and therefore have different, and higher expectations of the social media platforms that we interact with on a daily basis.

For Gen-Z, how a brand carries itself digitally is essential to their perception of a brand, and "Gen-Z understands that social media is actually bringing a brand to life." Brands need to create an image, and a "whole personality" for their brand, and need to look at their social media from beyond just a marketing standpoint in order to resonate with younger audiences like Gen-Z.

Gen-Z expects this sort of transparency and personality in a campaign for any particular brand. We are "used to that level of intimacy and communication with brands," as well as influencers and celebrities that are promoting their favorite products, their own products, or even themselves on social media. This social media marketing, whether for a personal brand or for an actual product, makes what brands Gen-Z chooses a "much more personal choice."

When I asked Zhang what issues Gen-Z particularly cares about, she said that "equality continues to be something that future generations strive for." Social justice and a need for social change and intersectionality throughout every single field are common themes for Gen-Z. At the end of the day, we need to focus on making the world more equal and sustainable before anything else, and a lot of this responsibility falls within the older people, and the industry behind these older generations, as even seen in fashion and activities in our daily routines. Brands like *Vogue* know they need to be authentic with posts about social justice and social change because there's a difference between brands that just pretend to care about equality and the brands that actually do, and Gen-Zers can pick up on a lack of authenticity.

Maria Bobila

Always. Logged. On. Three words that Maria Bobila, the fashion editor at Nylon, says define Gen-Z as a generation, because Gen-Z's life experience is so ingrained with social media and the internet. The hardest part of a job like Maria's is the constant need to be on social media and never miss a beat. She needs to keep up with the constantly changing world, be familiar with the slang and lingo used on social media and needs to keep her audience in mind when looking for and writing content.

Maria's role as fashion editor requires her to use social media as a resource for content ideas, doing deep dives on TikTok, Instagram, and Twitter threads in order to find the next best story. Maria and her team report on aesthetics or trends that pop on TikTok, highlight shops and business owners from Depop, and do shopping roundups that appeal to Gen-Z's sartorial interests, which usually involves researching what Gen-Z's favorite influencers/celebrities are wearing on social media.

In today's world, and specifically with Gen-Z, social media is everything, so it is unsurprising that social media has transformed the world of fashion as well. Maria says that Gen-Z specifically is more in-tune with what's considered #spon (sponsored) and advertising and don't put up with it, so influencers have to do a really good job of loving and promoting their interest in the brand to make their partnerships seem authentic.

What does Gen-Z want from the fashion industry specifically?
- low-cost, picture-worthy looks that drive up interaction on their social media feeds
- sustainability
- unique, on-trend looks that show personality

Social media has also "democratized the industry" according to Bobila. Consumers are more informed, but they're also given so much information at once, so it's important for designers to be authentic and tell a good story in order to stand out in social media.

Doin' it for the 'gram: If you haven't heard of that phrase, it means doing a particular action (most commonly taking a picture) for Instagram, or an Instagram account. Bobila says that "Social media plays a bigger role in fashion choices for Gen-Z compared to other generations. They're more open to expressing their individuality through style and are so much more informed as a shopper/consumer. Also, they consume fashion in such a different way compared to older generations. We were notified about trends and what to shop through magazines, television, retailer catalogs, and going to the mall. Thanks to social media, a Gen-Zer has SO many more resources when it comes to discovering fashion."

Looking picture perfect is something I can even attest to. Sometimes, I go to the store and buy an outfit with a particular location for a photo in mind, or even purchase a piece that might only look good in a picture and be unreasonable for normal wear. But the hard part is not wearing a particular piece too many times on your social media feed, because after a while, it looks repetitive.

Sustainability is the new standard: Brands are also finding new ways to appeal to Gen-Z, with more brands focusing on a social good component to their brand and also a new focus on sustainability. A lot of brands are upcycling or using deadstock fabrics or natural dyes. Pre-order is becoming popular as a means of keeping production waste low, and secondhand shopping is becoming much more commonplace.

Save that dough: Gen-Z is looking for "secondhand shopping, thrifting, sustainability, DIY fashion, customization, and outfits that look good in photos" according to Bobila, and that "Gen-Z is definitely looking for more unique pieces when it comes to fashion, whether that's through customization or scouring thrift stores for a one-of-a-kind item." Gen-Z also has a lot of options to choose from when it comes to their choices in clothing, because "as Millennials really only had Zara, H&M, and Forever 21, Gen-Z has way, way more choices/websites to shop from." These retailers allow for Gen-Zers to buy picture-perfect outfits for a small cost. For me, this means buying cheaper or secondhand clothing that is less expensive so that I can have more, for less.

Bobila says that in terms of picking up stories to write about, she "tries to trust her gut as much as possible." This is a sentiment to the Gen-Z attitude of following through on what you want rather than what you think society wants. With Gen-Z, there isn't as much of a responsibility towards what is right or wrong when moving forwards; it's more about you and your internal compass and seeing if that sticks with other people. Bobila says that "Sometimes I may be interested in covering something that hasn't been covered before in mainstream media. I try to not let that deter me because chances are that's what will make your stories stand out."

Matt Sarafa

Fashion is an industry that is sometimes overlooked in its value to shape society. I got to interview Matt Sarafa, who is the youngest designer to have ever shown at New York, Los Angeles, and Paris fashion weeks. Sarafa has dressed several celebrities from supermodels, to pop stars, to actors, and even reality TV stars! Some of the most notable people who Sarafa has dressed include Tyra Banks, Doja Cat and Iggy Azalea. Fashion is a transformative force that incites empowerment, because as Sarafa says, "There is no better feeling in the world to me than putting on an outfit that you *know* you look and feel good in, then going about your day feeling like a total badass," which goes to show the power of a good outfit and good design.

As Sarafa says, "Fashion is such a powerful and underrated force." He explained how diversity and authenticity were paramount pillars to his brand. Matt Sarafa got a very early start in fashion and started designing when he was just seven years old after watching a marathon of *Project Runway*. In a couple of years, Sarafa was competing on *Project Runway Junior*. Even though Sarafa didn't win the show, he was given a new platform to get started on his career in fashion. From there, Sarafa's career grew at a rapid pace, and his dream of launching a clothing line happened before his seventeenth birthday. Most teenagers (including myself) feel lucky to have made it through high school by seventeen or eighteen, but Matt Sarafa did it all; and he's currently the CEO of both his apparel and accessory lines, which fall under the umbrella of his company Matt Sarafa LLC.

Matt Sarafa got a young start, which had its advantages and disadvantages. Sarafa says that his youth gives him "fresh perspective" in the fashion industry and allows him to cater his brand to the ever-evolving market. However, Sarafa also says that being young has its cons because if someone older takes interest in someone with little to no experience in one of their endeavors, it's much easier to be taken advantage of. Sarafa said that "When (he) was sixteen getting ready to launch (his) first fashion line after *Project Runway Junior*, so many older 'experts' were coming out of the woodworks offering to guide and help (him), only to find out they were really screwing (him) over to make a quick buck." This is a common narrative that many young and successful entrepreneurs, business owners, activists, and more experience when first starting out.

For Sarafa, "Diversity is *everything.*" Sarafa is openly gay and describes himself as being "a little more flamboyant than most," but uses his unique personality to be inclusive through his brand. On his website, there are no labels of a traditional men's or women's section, as Sarafa believes that "fashion shouldn't have any labels, and if you like something you should feel free to rock it." By showing this diversity through his brand, Sarafa is able to appeal to several different audiences and provide an open environment where fashion is fashion, no matter who you are.

This leads into the importance of authenticity in fashion, specifically in Sarafa's brand. Sarafa says that "without authenticity, you have nothing to stand on." He noted that "our generation has amazing BS detectors and can spot inauthenticity from a mile away," which is not only important to note for his brand and brand strategy, but even for all of us, and our "personal brands" that we move forward with on social media.

Many older brands believe that there is a loss of personal connection when advertising and marketing on social media, but Sarafa believes the contrary. To him, "Social media marketing feels a little more personal and casual as opposed to traditional marketing which feels a little contrived and dated." Social media according to Sarafa is a marketing tool that makes resources accessible and easy to use, which is perfect for new and small businesses. Sarafa attributes some of his brand's success to Instagram, as he is able to reach hundreds of thousands of people in a few clicks and do it all for free.

Sarafa's one piece of advice? "We hold the power to change the world. Don't let anyone or anything stop you from making your dreams come true because trust me, it'll be worth it."

Jasmine Cheng

Shoes have lately started to become more of a fashion statement than functional. People take a lot of pride in their shoe collections and are willing to take enormous risks and spend large amounts of money in order to get the shoes that they want. Jasmine Cheng finds shoes for high-profile clients, in their desired style and color, to get them the shoe of their dreams.

Jasmine is going to be a freshman at Rutgers University in 2020, but already has her successful business up and running. A Gen-Zer herself, her client list already includes celebrities like Lamar Jackson, Jalen Ramsey, Metro Boomin, DK Metcalf, and Joey Badass. She said what inspired her to start her business was her passion for shoes. She saw an opportunity to turn it into a business and took it!

However, this journey was not easy for her, because "At first, many people did not necessarily trust (her) since (she) had no reputation or clientele they could refer to." Being a woman and a teenage young woman in the business was no easy feat either. Jasmine "struggled a little more than the other typical males in the industry." A lot of athletes (some of her top clientele) were skeptical to answer or reach out because of (her) gender.

Jasmine says that keys to her success were sticking to her principles of being ethical, reliable, and accessible.

Jasmine also says that being reliable, available, and having communication with her clients is essential to any client relationship because they need to know what they are paying for. This ties back to Gen-Z's need to be real and authentic with those that they interact with.

Jasmine says that for her, communication is key, and this is a necessary skill in the social media age. For starters, one must choose their words wisely, and make sure that they say what they mean to say because 1) there are a lot of ways that statements can be misinterpreted, so clarity is key, and 2) once something is on the internet and social media, it never goes away. This is something to keep in mind, especially with businesses because they must have a certain code of conduct, and also good communication skills because they might not be interacting directly with their clients, but rather via social media.

Building her reputation is essential for Jasmine because it also allows for her clientele to trust her. Jasmine makes sure that she gets references and shoutouts on her page to boost this reputation and add to her reliability. There are tons of websites that are set up online that offer services like Jasmine's but turn out to be scams.

When Jasmine started her business, and even still to this day, she always hears the term "clout chaser," where people are accusing her of doing what she does for fame and connections. What people don't understand is that without those connections that Jasmine worked to build, she wouldn't have been able to achieve her success.

When I asked Jasmine what she thinks that Gen-Z specifically wants in fashion, she said "anything that people hype up. There is no set style anymore." This goes to show the power of trends in the social media age, how one has the need to participate in these trends and have the trendy product or style before the fad is over, and to make a post on their social media page. People also carefully curate their social media feeds to fit their particular aesthetic, and the right products make the page.

Today, people want to look like famous people, and the people that are getting the likes. Jasmine says that "I think whatever you see celebrities wear nowadays is what you want to wear, or at least that seems to be the trend, with brands like Off-White, Palm Angels, anything Travis Scott related. Really again, whatever celebrities wear." Products of brands that are backed by popular influencers have products sold out the day after they are released, like the popular YouTuber and beauty influencer James Charles's makeup palette that sold out just ten minutes after it was released.[50]

Specifically in the shoe game, people spend so much because they want to "have drip," meaning looking cool or having

50 Denise Curtin, "James Charles' Morphe palette sells out in less than 10 minutes after going on sale," *Her,* November 13, 2018.

something to show off. Shoes have become a popular way for people to express themselves. People wait for specific releases to be on top of the game. They want to have the newest shoes before the majority of people. People also take care of their purchases because of the resell value of many shoes, specifically more exclusive releases.

Shoes are considered to be prized possessions to many, similar to cars. The newly released Air Jordan 1 Dior collaboration only released six thousand pairs of shoes, and one of these pairs goes for more than $30,000, more than some new cars! People also buy so many shoes, because "collecting shoes can become addicting. NIKE and all those brands are constantly coming out with new ones, so it makes you feel like you have to always be buying."

According to Cheng, Gen-Z in particular has a higher affinity to the shoe game. She says that the "rise in hype shoes has been undeniable. It has become a way to express oneself. So many young adults and children have dipped their feet (no pun intended) into the shoe business as well... which I think will only continue to skyrocket." To Cheng, Gen-Z are "her customers!" They are the ones who truly care and know about shoes and hype. Cheng says that "People like my parents could care less what brand or style" of shoes that they are wearing.

Kristina Ang

Kristina Ang is a Parsons student who started off wanting to go into STEM. However, Kristina was able to merge her interests and find herself in her true passion: fashion.

Kristina's insights were interesting as she brought a perspective of a student in the fashion field and is a Gen-Zer who is able to build on her interests and make them a reality. Kristina said that fashion was starting to become more intersectional, with more career options opening up in the fashion industry intersecting with business, graphics, marketing, and more.

In today's world, everything is fast paced and changing every second. With so much similarity out there in the market, it's hard for brands to establish themselves. This is where the fashion industry becomes interesting. Here are four things that Kristina talked to me about.

- Influencers
- Using unconventional materials like deadstock fabrics, or even algae
- Focusing on sustainability as a counter to fast fashion
- Using outlets like Depop and Instagram to create an audience, ground up.

Influencers hold influence. With thousands to hundreds of thousands of followers, influencer marketing is a great way for companies to give free or discounted products for influencers to style or post about on their social media feeds and gain business from their following that wants to purchase or have the same items. Strategic influencer partnerships can be extremely beneficial for brands and can make people see the products on people that they know and have followed for a while versus traditional models that would show the particular pieces or items. Kristina herself could be considered an influencer with partnerships with Inkbox, True and Co, Casely, and more.

I mentioned at the beginning of this chapter that fashion is at the intersection of almost every other field. Fashion isn't just using cloth anymore. Scarlett Yang, "a recent graduate from acclaimed London design school Central Saint Martins, developed a high-fashion dress made from silk cocoon protein and algae extract. This textile is completely biodegradable."[51] This dress even dissolves in water after use. Designers like Yang are using unconventional materials like algae to set themselves apart from other designers, and to move into a more sustainable world of fashion, accessible for all.

Using different materials, including deadstock, not only creates a sustainable image for the designer, but it also allows for a buyer to buy into sustainability. Sustainability is a big part of fashion in the future because Gen-Zers want to be a part of a new movement for change and want our clothing to reflect this. A lot of Gen-Zers are also aware of fast fashion, which "is a design, manufacturing, and marketing method focused on rapidly producing high volumes of clothing. Garment production utilizes trend replication and low-quality materials in order to bring inexpensive styles to the public. These cheaply made, trendy pieces have resulted in an industry-wide movement towards overwhelming amounts of consumption. Unfortunately, this results in harmful impacts on the environment, garment workers, and, ultimately, consumers' wallets."[52]

Gen-Z cares. And although a lot of us are ready to purchase a cheap item of clothing to model on our Instagram feeds,

---

51 Lilly Smith, "The clothing of the future completely dissolves after use," *Fast Company,* August 31, 2020.

52 Audrey Stanton, "What Is Fast Fashion, Anyway?" *The Good Trade,* October 8, 2018.

we're also starting to become more aware of what fast fashion is and what it means for the future of the world that we live in.

Using social media and selling on outlets like Depop is another way for Gen-Zers to access smaller fashion designers and for fashion designers to build an audience. Depop is essentially like eBay, with independent sellers typically selling used items or their own creations.

Let me provide you with a scenario. For example, I might be scrolling through my TikTok and find an influencer styling a new brand I've never heard of. I might click the tag of the brand's username (which is provided in a caption or description) and be directed to the brand's page. This is where I could see more of their pieces, or find their website, social media, or even Depop where I could see further examples of the clothes styled, and possibly buy any items that I would like.

This scenario displays how by seeing a particular style on someone else like an influencer, I could be influenced to easily purchase an item from this brand. And brands can have several iterations of these very interactions. For example, there is a whole selection of brands that sell on Instagram, and you can always link a store in your bio on any social platform. So, if I'm a seller myself with a lot of followers, anyone who views my page can easily click my website, Depop, or selling platform. Such platforms can not only drive up sales, but also create a community of people that are posting about and viewing certain brands and products online.

Influencer marketing, sustainability, and constantly changing trends are only a few of the ideas explored in this chapter.

As Lucie Zhang said, fashion trends are an indication of culture—a culture that's formed primarily by youth and Gen-Zers. In terms of predicting what Gen-Z will resonate with, or even predicting something as small as the color scheme in a new campaign at a company, take a peek at fashion trends, and what's popular. I'll give you a quick example: sage green and brown. Two colors, relatively ordinary. Except, Gen-Z is kind of obsessed with both colors to the point where there were mood boards and aesthetics based on the two colors. Brands that paid attention would be able to use hashtags like #sagegreen or #brown to boost their content. Brands that paid attention used variations of the two colors in their products and marketing. Brands that paid attention captured the eye of the new Gen-Z consumer.

Chapter 9

Decisions, and performative ones too.

────

Decision-making—it's different

There are so many options in today's world—making it harder to choose. We're an "interdependent" generation, with a "greater need for approval" with every decision we make.[53] And the major life decisions that affect where we are going to go and who we are going to be are put out on social media, for potentially hundreds or thousands of people to view. This sets up another societal pressure to make the right decision, and that impacts Gen-Z. Gen-Z is the "product of the unique, interconnected, interdependent environment in which its members were raised" and when making decisions, Gen-Z "can be distracted by their emotions or other factors" which can lead to indecisiveness.[54]

---

53 Jason McDowell, "Is Generation Z Too Interdependent–or Is That the Future of Work?" recruiter.com, November 21, 2016.

54 Ibid.

It is prudent to include the fact that some of what I'm saying has to do with age, and Gen-Z could learn with experience. But the best way to convey what Gen-Z is feeling through the seemingly endless options on any front—whether that be their next outfit purchase, or what they end up studying in college (or even going to college for that matter) is a menu. A long menu at that. Think about a really long menu at a restaurant, with all of the options being suitable, and rated ten-out-of-ten by reviewers and past diners at the restaurant. You'd have trouble picking, right? It makes a seemingly easy, or possible decision so much harder.

Now, add this to the mix. You want to pick something that is suitable to the palette but also looks good on Instagram. So, do you choose the tastier, unappetizing-looking dish, or the average-tasting Michelin-star presentation dish?

There are several different layers to the decision-making of Gen-Z. The restaurant example was very simplified, but down to even the clothes that a Gen-Zer puts on, everything is judged and looked upon. You almost have to continually edit yourself to the way that you want to present yourself to the world. We're impulsive in that way because we'll do anything to maintain that image. And although now, people are starting to get tired of keeping up the facade, the social pressures that social media inputs on an individual weigh on them in terms of making decisions.

Connor Blakely

Connor Blakely is regarded as the top authority for understanding the youth culture that is Gen-Z, and has worked with companies like Hasbro, the NHL, Sprint, PepsiCo, Johnson and Johnson and more. And that's just on his website.

I got to talk to Connor on a relatively new social media-esque platform centered around true, unedited conversation called Clubhouse. I opened up a room on the app, and we got to talk about who he is, what he's doing, and where he's going.

When Connor was fourteen, he realized that he wanted to find a way to work with big brands but saying that he wanted to run their social media wasn't cutting it. So, after hearing companies tell him that he was too young, Connor decided to use that very rhetoric to his advantage. Connor was one of the first people to coin terms like "Gen-Z marketer" or "Gen-Z entrepreneur" after researching and looking into who Gen-Z is and what we're looking for. After this research, Connor was able to start a company at fifteen called YouthLogic. From there he spoke internationally and worked with those very big brands that had labeled him as "too young" before.

Hearing this was amazing, and in reality, Connor's work inspired a lot of other young entrepreneurs and young people in general to get involved in the Gen-Z space. But in true fashion, I was curious; why was talking to big companies about Gen-Z vital to the company's success? The obvious facts are that Gen-Z would be companies' next main consumer base, but Connor's answer to this question was interesting. He said,

> *"Gen-Z is a customer segment that controls culture. You can't measure culture because it's so fundamentally based on perception and preeminence, which you can't really quantify quantitatively."*

Now that quote is full of impact. When Connor said that in the interview, my reaction was, "yeah, that's straight facts." But let's break that down. The Gen-Z consumer segment is so vast. But wait. What does consumer segment mean?

> According to CMG Consulting, **consumer segmentation** is the practice of dividing a customer base into groups of individuals that are similar in specific ways relevant to marketing, such as age, gender, interests, and spending habits.[55]

So now that that's covered, think about it. If you can understand Gen-Z, in a way, you can control culture. You can influence the things that everyone is talking about, the new hype, the new trends, and really just all of the above. So, if you still aren't sold on why you should read this book, there it is.

But, back to Connor. When I asked about why Gen-Z is so into authenticity and being their true selves, Connor simply said "we don't know how to operate any other way." He continued in addressing the fact that people can make the argument that on social media people can put up fake images of themselves and make things up, but that can get exposed. Connor said that "social media is an incubator for real-world engagement and real-life connections. So, we're forced to operate in way of maybe not even who we are, but an amplification of who we want to be, which is so authentic."

---

55 "How Consumer Segmentation Helps Your Marketing Goals," *CMG Consulting*, November 10, 2020.

There's another wow statement. But what motivates and drives Gen-Z to behave and act in such a way? To Connor, it's all about self-interest. Now, this is interesting. And I recognize that the book so far has been in the message that "Gen-Zers are changemakers." However, Gen-Zers like attention and are also very particular about messaging and how we come off based on our social media profiles. So, we might end up doing things that we don't even want to particularly do but match our Instagram aesthetic. I've gone to coffee shops or trendy restaurants where I wouldn't normally step foot, but because the place is so hype—or because posting a picture of the food at that restaurant/coffee shop would look good on my Instagram—I end up going (and usually end up paying a lot more for it).

Now, let's take this very concept and apply it to a lens of social good and social change. After the events in 2020 with George Floyd (Floyd was unjustly asphyxiated as police officers arrested him for allegedly using a counterfeit bill) and the movement that resulted after, a trend on social media went around, to post a black square to stand as allies with the #blacklivesmatter movement. Now everyone did this, whether you supported the cause or didn't. And honestly, it was weird if you didn't.

This is where the notion of performative activism comes into play. A lot of people post activist resources and information on their social media, just for show and for the optics, without much intent behind the particular posting. So, in the case of posting the black square in solidarity, a lot of people posted the square, but behind the scenes on their private stories or closer-knit networks said the n-word or disagreed with what was going on. So, in a lot of cases, we're lacking impact-driven social good, but rather taking part in social good simply because it "looks good."

So, is it opportunistic to say that Gen-Z is the changemaker generation? Possibly. But it goes without saying that there are more people faking it than making the change we need. Is my perspective as an author jaded because I'm from a strongly liberal state and have been raised in a diverse, liberal town? Definitely. But it would be wrong for me to write a book about Gen-Z and give you only what I think. Like Connor said in my conversation with him, it'd be wrong to put earbuds in and tune people out.

Back to Gen-Z. We're doing stuff. From starting companies at age fourteen like Connor to redefining traditional spaces, we're doing it all. But why? It's because we have access to more information and technology at a very rapid pace in the formative psychological years of our brain development. Simply, we have access to resources sooner. And because we've been raised with the internet, we can figure things out quicker. We don't have to memorize mundane facts like who built the Lincoln Memorial or who the mayor of our town is because we can look that information up in less than a second.

When I asked Connor about empathy, he said that Gen-Z has way too much empathy—to the point where people start trying to have empathy for themselves. It's great to talk about our emotions and the things we've gone through. However, like Connor mentioned in our interview, some people just talk about how disenfranchised they are and how their life sucks, but nothing comes out of it. Essentially, there's a lot of talk without any action, and a lot of times this type of conversation can have a time and place, but a lot of times, it can be used as a ploy for attention and sympathy.

Frank and straightforward are two words that I would use to describe my conversation with Connor. The best part about our conversation was how well-rounded it was and not shrouded in a particular perspective. Connor addressed the fact that some of his answers could sound pessimistic, but he said that we need to stop "perpetuating a false reality" and that "if we don't address the reality of the situation it's hard to progress."

Connor is only twenty-one years old and already breaking into the alcohol industry, starting the company BRU brands. So, the hardest part of his job? Measuring and managing stress and figuring out the right balance between relationships and business. Want to read more about that? Go back to **yup... tech has its downsides** and go down to the section about a blurred line between work and home.

> *There has never been a better, less costly and more needed time to be a social entrepreneur. Thanks to the combination of cloud computing and social media, the cost of failure is one tenth what it was a decade ago. As a result, Gen-Z can now afford to bring their dream social enterprises to life from bedrooms and garages across the globe. The time for change is now, and it's just one click away.*
>
> —JENK OZ, THRED MEDIA

Chapter 10

Talk to us, not about us

They are a lot of assumptions made about Gen-Z because we are younger, and our power is undermined. We aren't considered up to par with the rest of the world even though we can offer insights and perspectives that might not have previously been considered.

By talking to us, one is able to obtain a unique perspective into the generation, and we can move forward not only for change, but for intergenerational equity. In this section, I got to talk to Sophia Delrosario, the founder of the Zenerations Instagram account, Ziad Ahmed, the co-founder and CEO of JUV consulting, and Neal Sivadas, a senior strategist at JUV consulting.

But first, let's talk about jobs.
We've seen our parents lose money. We've seen our parents without jobs. We've seen our parents unsatisfied with their lives and how they're leading them.

We want to be different.

When it comes to the job market, Gen-Z is looking for security, and also potentially having several jobs at a time or changing jobs frequently. This is for a few reasons:

- The job market is moving at a rapid pace. You might be totally secure as a construction worker in 2021. However, in a few years when robots can do the bulk of construction work, what will you end up doing? Now this scenario isn't just applicable in construction. Technology is changing the job landscape, and Gen-Z needs to keep up with it to survive. What's relevant and in demand today might not be the same tomorrow.

- We want to be satisfied with our jobs and what we do. We've seen our parent's generation grovel around and work where they have to in order to make ends meet. With the resources that we have, Gen-Z is able to capitalize on our passions, turning them into viable careers that we actually love. And the beautiful thing about working remotely (as a lot of jobs are mainly online based) is that you could have a couple jobs that you love equally. I could be an influencer doing brand deals and making money via sponsorships, but also be a graphic designer, channeling a love for art. In today's day and age, being a creative isn't looked down upon anymore.

And let me elaborate on working remotely. Although one might think of sitting in a house or an apartment, there are a lot of benefits to working online from being able to travel and take Zoom calls from a beach, to being able to create your own work schedule with a more reasonable routine with constructive breaks like workouts or healthy eating. Of course, this is all when we are not living in a pandemic.

Essentially, Gen-Z wants to be satisfied with what we're doing in our careers. There are opportunities galore, and we can create our own futures at the very touch of our fingertips.

Sophia Delrosario—Zenerations

With sixty-three thousand followers and growing, Sophia Delrosario has created a space for Gen-Z teens to learn about issues that are going on in the world, that affect them, and to harness this knowledge moving forward in their lives. With people like Alexandria Ocasio-Cortez (better known as AOC) following the account, and people like Ariana Grande posting graphics from the account to her story, Zenerations has been able to accurately assess what is relevant, make content on such topics, and create a loyal following that stays updated with the account.

For Sophia, Zenerations has filled that "void inside (her) as a creative outlet and allowed (her) to further develop and furnish (her) skills as a leader and as a creative and as an artist," and this is what social media platforms can do for Gen-Z: help them explore who they are.

Sophia is the director and founder of Zenerations and uses her role to find and curate a team with unique talents and distinctive abilities. However, without social media, this account-turned-community would never have existed, and this is something Sophia recognizes. She says that prior to Zenerations, and prior to a rise in social activism, she, along with most people, would log on to social media platforms in order to stay updated with other people in her life, see their pictures, and see what they were doing on a particular day. This is what Instagram and other social platforms formerly were.

However, now such platforms have turned into a source of news, a way for people to communicate information to each other, and a place to learn about things that are affecting ourselves and those that we care about. We are slowly pushing toward more digital activism and digital education. With social media platforms coming out with shorter mediums of information like TikTok, reels on Instagram, and a limited amount of slides on an Instagram carousel post, people make informative posts and content to the point and easy to understand for maximum impact.

Something unique about Zenerations is its signature blue hues, which give off a calm and relaxing graphic in the sea of crazy that is social media. This color scheme in addition to the style in which the graphics are drawn make it easier for Gen-Z to understand the information and be more open to actually learning and absorbing the information. Gen-Z has a large age range, and in order to cater to the entire diaspora of Gen-Z, the graphics need to be identifiable and consistent for the viewer to be able to clearly see that a particular graphic is from the Zenerations account.

Zenerations has sometimes come under fire for the controversial nature of some of its content. However, Sophia says that one shouldn't be afraid to say and put out controversial information as long as you have sources that are backed up and as long as you know you're not spreading misinformation, which is extremely common in the social media world. However, not only do Sophia and her team tackle controversy with the facts, but she also uses her platform for social good, fundraising for nonprofits and working with other accounts to create events for her account's community.

Sophia described Gen-Z as the "changemaker generation," and emphasized the importance of releasing inhibitions and going after what one loves. Sophia talked about how when she first started the account, she didn't see any relevant information about the events and happenings that she and her friends talked and knew about. Once she started acting on this, she realized and learned that this was something that others lacked as well. She brought in other Gen-Zers that were passionate and got them to work with her to create the content that she produces on the account.

When I asked Sophia what the hardest thing about her role in Zenerations was, she answered in one word: burnout. This is a common theme with Gen-Z, and many inspirational projects and accounts similar to Zenerations are student-led, which makes it harder to manage both one's student life and life outside of it. Sophia also mentioned how she is a perfectionist, and although it helps her, it can also be painful in terms of the expectations of social media.

Zenerations is the epitome of the name of this chapter: talk to us, and not about us. Sophia and her international team work to make content that truly matters to Gen-Z and are regarding topics Gen-Z cares about. As a result, Zenerations' content is one of the first posts and accounts shown when searching #genz on Instagram. Accounts like Zenerations are able to gain a following because they are able to understand what Gen-Z wants and are by Gen-Zers themselves.

Sophia was recently hired after this interview as an Insights Strategist at JUV consulting (learn about this company more in the next section); a position that requires Sophia to rely on her pulse for what's trending and what's hot within Generation Z, incorporating this into a live database that acts as a widespread company resource and supporting the social media team and client projects. Sophia is currently the youngest member of the JUV leadership at only sixteen years old. This new role of Sophia's just goes to show how capable Gen-Z is in terms of innovating and making their way into the world.

At only sixteen, Sophia is a student, manages her job with JUV consulting, and runs the Zenerations account. If you haven't gathered that Sophia is amazing, she says that she's embracing her true self as someone who embodies every aspect of the youth and social media.

Something unique about JUV (which I promise I'm getting to) is the corporate culture. JUV is on its way to becoming a Fortune 500 company, and there are several other Gen-Z marketing companies that are opening, trying to capitalize on the Gen-Z audience. But what makes JUV different? Sophia says that the team always welcomes her with an unmatched, crazy yet cool energy, a certain company quality that you don't get to see in every corporate group.

When I talked to Sophia, she only had the job for a few weeks, but she says that she's found a family in JUV consulting. Why do I include this? Well, as Gen-Z starts to become leaders in their field, CEOs of their business ventures, and important people in general, we cultivate a collaborative and interesting workspace culture where there's no judging—no matter who you are, how old you are, how you identify, or where you come from, you're welcome in the working culture. This is different, and this is what makes Gen-Z different, even in the corporate world.

Ziad Ahmed and JUV consulting

The wait is over. Here, I talk about JUV consulting and its founder, Ziad Ahmed.

Dynamic. Informed. Inspirational. These three words aptly describe Ziad Ahmed. Just talking to this young CEO is awe-inspiring, and his energy makes you want to start brainstorming the next Fortune 500 company right at that very moment.

Ziad is the CEO and co-founder of JUV consulting. JUV consulting is a Gen-Z agency and consulting company where clients come to the company to figure out how to better market, understand, and reach young people. A reason why Ziad's company is successful? The receipt network behind it. I'm a member of the receipt network. The receipt network involves Gen-Zers, like me, taking short surveys based on information that brands JUV consulting works with want to know about Gen-Z. That way, JUV is able to provide the companies it works with the most accurate and current "temperature" of Gen-Z, and what we want and need.

Beyond the basic LinkedIn profile, Ziad values one word: diversity. Applying to college, Ahmed wrote "BlackLivesMatter" one hundred times as one of his Stanford college essays, and got in. On that same note, as a CEO, Ahmed says that it's his job "to grow the business, but to make sure that we're staying true to our values and to cultivate a culture and a community that I'm really proud of and I feel really grateful to do the work that I do." He describes his team and company as "partners, thought leaders, and problem solvers, that push society forward," continuing to say that the "products, campaigns, and ideas" that he works with "actually resonate with young people with purpose and with meaning." "When diverse young people have this chance to thrive, and people give us a space to thrive we thrive."

JUV is a team of majority women, majority people of color, and a significant share queer. Ziad says that "when you have a bunch of diverse minds and a lot of people who historically are in the business world, we shake things up and we do business differently; we do it better." Now that seems like a lot, but there's more. But before I move on, I wanted to add that I only had fifteen minutes with Ziad but got a lifetime's worth of information.

As I asked Ziad what inspired him to start JUV, he said that there were youth experts who are fifty years old consulting on Gen-Z, and all he could think about was how Gen-Z could speak for themselves. He said that other generations' mechanisms of understanding us are broken, and he needed to find a way to fix that. So as a high schooler at his desktop, Ziad started his company.

When I asked about what sets JUV consulting apart, Ziad simply answered, "JUV comes from a real place of purpose and we exist to empower young people; we try to engage in impact on purpose through every campaign and every internal decision on all our socials." For more context, JUV consulting has worked with big brands like Levi's, Viacom, and Unilever, and has been featured on *Business Insider, Forbes, NPR, Vice, BBC, The New York Times,* and *Today.*

Like many other Gen-Z leaders, Ziad **goes to school while running his business.** Ziad is a student at Yale University and says that there's never enough hours in a day. Beyond being a good student and CEO, Ziad also said that he wanted to be a good friend, son, brother, and good human. So, juggling everything and maintaining boundaries in every field of life is essential.

In terms of working with and around Gen-Z all the time, Ziad said that "people forget we're human," and often look at Gen-Z like a different species. But what he said Gen-Z valued is probably one of the most valuable insights from talking to him. "Manifesting authenticity is particularly important to Gen-Z because we've grown up in such an oversaturated media landscape, so there's so much content out there, and we need things that cut through the noise." Gen-Z doesn't care about the petty information and the "noise" because we have an internalized BS filter to cut through it. Our attention is diverted to the "bigger fish to fry," in terms of longer-term problems and viable solutions to address such dilemmas. Gen-Z has free internet capital, all around the world instantaneously, to learn about their struggles and the struggles of others, and we have so much content to choose from. And so much opportunity to make content.

Even as Gen-Z browses social media, we use it differently. It's not just a communication platform for us, but we're using it for whatever gets us closer to our goal. For a lot of us, that means connecting with people from all around the world who share our common interest to build solutions together. Connecting to people all around the world means that we can find common ground and build off of the notions that we're actually more similar than different, and that we can resonate with people instantaneously because we actually all share a lot of our different dimensions. As Ziad said, "We're not beautiful because we're the same and all the same color, we're beautiful because of our many colors."

Gen-Z uses social media, but this is underscored because we use it to really build community and capacity and to push ourselves and the world forward. Like many other interviews in this book, intersectionality was discussed when I talked to Ziad. "You can't talk about climate change without talking about environmental racism without talking about income inequality without talking about discriminatory housing laws without talking about homophobia." Everything is connected, intersected, and even looking inward to Gen-Z. As many people identify as people of color, gender noncon- forming, and queer, we're starting to understand the intersec- tionality of our own identities and how they relate to others.

When I asked Ziad what issues matter to Gen-Z, he answered: "The polling and data would suggest that we care about climate change, mental health, gun violence, and systemic racism. As we go through waves and life, different things become top of mind, but in general, we understand all these things are connected." Intersectionality is who we are becoming and who we are going to be as a generation.

I asked Ziad to define Gen-Z in three words, as an expert in the field. But he said he couldn't answer. Why? "Because I think people think it's easy to pretend that there's three words, I could define two billion people on Pinterest. And they are not all the same, we're different. We live in all sorts of corners around the world, and face different problems in different circumstances, and have different perspectives. It's easy to group people together and think that we all market the same way but it's not how the world works. Gen-Z is not a monolith, and don't treat us like one."

Young people are the ones who often have the hard conversations and push society forward. What's special about Gen-Z is, we have the digital resources to allow such disruptions to become mainstream. Our power is profound, and we're able to use digital tools to control popular culture and public discourse. Gen-Z shows up and shows out. In ten or twenty years, Ziad said that "I see us having fundamentally changed the business world, the marketplace, and nonprofit world in politics forever. By bringing in more programs, by bringing in more diverse leaders, by championing intersectionality. I see this hopefully creating a world that is kind to the kids of Generation Z."

Neal Sivadas

Neal Sivadas is a USC student who is already a senior strategist at JUV consulting and the author of the *Find Gen Z* series.

Neal told me that he was interning at a marketing agency and realized that a lot of people don't really understand who Gen-Z is. There's a lot written about us, a lot of statistics, and a lot of data, but there really isn't actual representation of who Gen-Z is. We aren't talked to, and we're not asked for our opinions. And this makes it really hard for the world to understand who Gen-Z is.

Neal wanted to bridge that gap. So, he created a newsletter on LinkedIn called the *Find Gen Z* series which documents how Gen-Z uses various social and digital media platforms and how to advertise them. This series now has three thousand subscribers, and this number is constantly growing. Neal is also a part of JUV consulting, headed by Ziad Ahmed. This opportunity allowed for Neal to start advising CEOs and CMOS on how to advertise and how to market to Gen-Z.

When I talked to Neal about what the hardest part of his job was, he said that it is to provide *actionable value*. He says that marketing is all about **quantifiable impact**: impact that can be quantified or measured. In order to be successful, you need to speak to marketers about what they should be doing, and how to do it. Throughout Neal's articles, his series, and his role at JUV consulting, he has been able to ensure that this delivery is up to par and to continue to have actionable value being provided for Gen-Z.

Neal said that this was only achievable through intergenerational equity. No other generation prior to Gen-Z has grown up consuming thousands of pieces of content every single day, and no generation has seen its institutions like government and schools crumble and struggle and be broken down throughout their childhood. However, we also haven't been in the workforce for decades, and don't have a whole lot of lived experience. But older generations do.

Okay, so based on that last paragraph, older generations bring something to the table, and so do Gen-Zers. The question beckons, how can we bring both sides together? The answer would be reverse mentoring. (Why does this matter? Read more in *Collective Trauma, and Bridging Generations*.) An article put out by *Insperity* explains this concept well. According to the article, "When we think of mentoring, we tend to think of seasoned employees taking younger employees under their wings and teaching them the ins and outs of business. Reverse mentoring flips the script. It's designed to empower younger workers to share *their* expertise and ideas with more senior employees." And although this is true, it can go both ways, where younger workers teach older workers their expertise, and vice versa. The benefits of this approach are full-fledged as well. Insperity lists five:[56]

- Bringing fresh perspective to your company
- Empower emerging leaders
- Sharpen the saw, and keep it sharp
- Teach new workers critical business survival skills
- Break down generational stereotypes

---

56   Lisa Jasper, "Reverse mentoring: 5 key reasons your business needs it," *Insperity.*

Now let me break each of these ideas down. Let's start off with:

1) Fresh perspective

Today's workplace has changed drastically. Whether that means a more open-concept office design from the traditional cubicles or the increased use of computers from the days of papers and pencils, older employees can learn from Gen-Zers that have grown up with technology. As mentioned with JUV, our work environments are more inclusive and "social in nature." This knowledge "can help bridge the gaps more seasoned staff may have, particularly in areas like social media and your business's online presence."[57]

"Reverse mentors will often become internal ambassadors for improving efficiency throughout your entire organization, for instance:"

- Leveraging technology to move from an outdated performance evaluation system to a digital platform
- Connecting to sales prospects using social media channels
- Developing multi-media marketing resources that incorporate podcasts and videos of customer testimonials
- Reducing expensive and unnecessary travel by adopting video conference technology and current mobile apps
- Collaborating with teams of diverse backgrounds and experiences

2) Empower emerging leaders

Older workers are big on company loyalty. Younger workers however "don't see themselves as tied by loyalty to any one company. Instead, what motivates them is how their work is valued, which makes reverse mentoring a great fit for them."[58]

---

57   Ibid.
58   Ibid.

To Gen-Zers, "nothing says, 'We value your skills and contribution to the company' quite like asking someone to share what they know, and coach and inspire others."

Reverse mentoring helps establish and strengthen relationships throughout a particular company, and makes employees feel more connected to one another. This connection is something that Gen-Zers are looking for: friends and coworkers who value them and their time as they come to work.

3) Sharpen the saw, and keep it sharp

"Lifelong learning is critical in today's workplace."[59] Any employee needs to stay updated in order to stay relevant. Fortunately for older workers, Gen-Zers are updated with all the new skills and can teach them to their older colleagues who are less experienced in new technology and innovations in the workplace. And in this mentorship, older workers can inform on how to advance such technology or use such innovations to one's advantage in a particular company workspace.

4) Teach new workers critical business survival skills

This is the time for senior employees to bring their skills to the table. Oftentimes, Gen-Zers are working while being in school, or fresh out of school. This transition is tough, and often not something that Gen-Zers are used to with limited experience working. So, senior employees "can share their deeper understanding of your company's cultural norms, inside information about how the business works, the right terminology to use when discussing a

---

59   Ibid.

business concept, and what and what not to do."[60] This provides Gen-Z employees with almost a "Workplace 101" crash course.

5) Break down generational stereotypes

Stereotypes are something that as a society, we have tried to break down, whether that be stereotypes associated with racism, sexism, ableism, or more. Generational stereotypes are something we continue to buy into, from deeming one generation as "stuck in the past" to another as "lazy." Reverse Mentoring is something we need to embrace in order to break down the often-overlooked generational stereotypes.

Generational stereotypes are statements we hear a lot. I've mentioned a few already, like how people think Gen-Zers are always on their phones and how we don't work as hard, whereas younger people think that older generations are generally very conservative, stuck in their opinions, and stubborn. Reverse mentoring allows for different generations to break out of the assumptions that society and generations themselves have set for other generations, and just embrace who people truly are, no matter what generation they're from. By better understanding one another and not looking at someone through the lens of their generation, we're able to build on each other's skillsets and assets in the workspace for a more inclusive and collaborative environment that benefits everyone and drives up profits and worker contentment.[61]

---

60 Ibid.
61 Ibid.

What's so different about us then?

So, back to Neal. He says that Gen-Z is built differently. We praise real people, real skin, and real ads. We grow up faster because we have ultimate exposure to anything and everything that we want to see. We talk about destigmatized topics. *We don't really want to sit at the table, we want to flip it.* We're ready to question the status quo and take action.

That was a lot of great one-liners, but there's meaning behind each of them. As you've read so far, Gen-Z has a passion to make change. But not only does this result in us seeing injustice, it's also about seeing these injustices earlier than ever before. Prior to Gen-Z, to be politically informed or aware of current events, you had to watch the news or read newspapers. And a lot of people didn't do that. Now, a simple notification on your phone can tell you about world events, from climate protests to women not getting paid the same as men.

Our news feeds have diversified, in terms of how global our content can be, but also narrowed down to show each and every one of us the content we are interested in and want to see. Like I stated earlier with Ava McDonald, authenticity is a driving force for Gen-Z. It's something we want to see because we don't want to have to hide behind our online personalities. We want to change the way that the world works because we've been hurt by it, and as of now, not that many people are listening to the valid concerns that we're raising.

What does successful mean in today's world?

When I talked to Neal about what he thinks makes content or posts that get a lot of views and likes, he says it's the fact that Gen-Z is native to the platform. We grew up on social media and know all the specific nuances and technicalities and formats for how to make the best video and make sure that it's appealing. We also have an understanding of what resonates with people.

So, whether that is education, humor, visual appeal, or creativity, we know what works and what people want because we're on these social media platforms every single day of our lives. Gen-Z also has relatability when it comes to content or posts. And that's what is getting them a lot of views and likes. We're creating a community on social media. So, these three things, in Neal's opinion, make content and posts get a lot of likes and interaction.

For Gen-Z, diversity and social good are penultimate. It's never a choice. No race makes up more than 50 percent of Gen-Z because we're the most diverse generation. Social media exposes us to other cultures and ideas. People are consciously and subconsciously, through our community, making content and expressing what they want to do. *We curate our social platforms to be a representation of we are and who we want to be.*

We grew up during a time when institutions have crumbled more than ever before, according to Neal. We see it as essential to solve the problems that may have been rampant throughout our childhood regarding healthcare, education, and government. And that becomes easy when you have dealt with the challenges that we have had to face. And this is what makes Gen-Z on particular social platforms different than other generations. That is why Gen-Z fights for the underrepresented and those that are less fortunate.

Neal told me that he portrays his own unique identity on social media and is able to find himself through doing so. He said that what's unique about a connected world is that you can choose how much you want to connect with your identity. Neal is Chinese and Indian-American, and there aren't a lot of people who share his identity. However, he's able to learn about "chindian" identity through social media and Facebook groups and still be in touch with aspects of his identity, even though it's not something that affects him on a day-to-day basis.

And this just goes to show how you can find support anywhere and everywhere from Gen-Zers all over the world from other community members. That is what Gen-Z leans on; they know that there are people out there just like them, and that makes us more connected as a generation.

Neal says that he developed his own personal brand and identity on different social platforms by putting his time into personal brand development on LinkedIn. He says that most of his professional accolades and updates remain on LinkedIn, and nonprofessional updates on other platforms, which allows him to draw a line between his professional and nonprofessional life. Neal suggests that you can't pinpoint successful social media accounts because social media means different things to different people. The very idea of social media is to connect people to communities that they are or want to be a part of. If you're helping or connecting with one person, you're already successful in Neal's opinion, which is very valid and something where we can see in the For-You Page. Your review page is created based off of creators that you liked or commented on or interacted with in some way, shape, or form.

So, for me, it could mean that I love to cook, and I love to be able to express myself through advocacy and writing; but for the person sitting right next to me with the same age, same nationality, same ethnicity, same race, same location, their FYP could be totally different because they might like certain things that I don't. So, their FYP could be filled with makeup, influencers, and fashion. And that's totally okay. We are two different people who want different things and want to see content based off of our interests.

Our FYPs are built differently, and to Neal's point, this really goes to show how diverse social media platforms are and are becoming. And if you're able to connect with even one person, then that's a connection that's worth something and is successful.

Gen-Z differs in comparison to other generations and their interactions and actions on social media, because Gen-Z creates, and according to Neal, other generations connect. If you think about a Millennial-founded social media platform like Facebook, Twitter, and LinkedIn, they are designed to connect and to stay in touch.

The most popular Millennial brands tend to focus on connecting with their customers, whether this means answering questions, spotlighting their customers, or even responding to posts, but the most popular Gen Z brands often have more personality. They create content to roast people and make them laugh and cry.

The best way to learn in Neal's opinion is by using the platforms that we are on every single day. And it's also interesting that he says that he takes a more critical eye to the platforms as he uses them. He always thinks about new features through the lens of "would this be part of a perfect social media platform?" You always have to stay one step ahead about our generation, and Neal says that he doesn't think about what people think is popular or trendy. He thinks about where people are going to go next. TikTok currently has the attention of Gen-Z for now, but that could change in a few years.

Two issues that Gen-Z particularly cares about or has an affinity to in Neal's opinion are representation and privacy. Gen-Z loves seeing strides in representation, especially in entertainment and politics. However, we will also stand up or vote for people based on their race. This isn't good or bad, but it's prevalent because we recognize societal constructs that have led to our thinking and we are educated about this every single day. We are able to recognize that we might need to change our thinking in order to be more equitable in the future.

Representation is extremely important for Gen-Z. The less fortunate and underrepresented, whether this is in healthcare or education or social justice, Gen-Z fights for. The fact that we're able to connect with people from all over the world allows us to put ourselves in the shoes of people who we might not ever have interacted with. We're able to gain these perspectives and understand where people are coming from, which builds our empathy, builds our values, and builds our responsibility as a generation to be representative and to understand the needs of everyone and work in some way, shape, or form to address them.

A willingness to compromise data privacy is another important issue that Gen-Z particularly cares about, according to Neal. Many other generations have concerns about data privacy, but Gen-Z is way more open to giving up their information because we've just been so used to doing that since we were very little. To Neal, what defines Gen-Z as generation is the context of our childhood. We are literally built different by it.

Gen-Z is definitely going to change work in Neal's opinion. Work in home and personal life used to be a dichotomy. But even as seen in this past year, this will change forever. The ways in which we present ourselves at work are much less strict than they used to be. Not to mention that we're the only generation to attend class and start working careers from our childhood bedrooms. Some companies have even created a permanent work from home policy, so this really redefined what it means to be professional, what it means to be present, and what it means to be at work. You could be wearing a great work shirt on top and be sitting on your chair in pajamas and be taking a call with a CEO, but this is the kind of life that Gen-Z is used to. We are taking school from our computers, and we are able to talk to our teachers and community leaders on a computer or phone. So, this allows us to understand that people are more than what they are at face value and move beyond that.

Neal also says that restrictions on social media etiquette for employees are going to be continually expanded. He says that imagine five years from now when a good portion of Gen-Z has entered the workforce, and the company has to review all the TikTok dance videos they had from a couple years back during our core team. There's going to be a much larger emphasis on can you get the job done, rather than the etiquette of showing up to work or the way that you present yourself.

And that's why Gen-Z really appeals to more authentic advertising. We don't want to be sold to or told what to do and conform to societal standards that we've been working for generations to break down. We want to relate, feel, create inertia, and be new and different in our views, our values, the content we interact with, and the content that we make. And that is why individuality and authenticity are so essential to Gen-Z. Gen-Z is an important and powerful generation to Neal because he thinks that we're the most badass generation ever. We're so creative, defiant, and relentless in our sight. With our desire for social change, he thinks, we're going to change the world, more than any other generation in history.

Chapter 11

The Gen-Z Dictionary

A disclaimer:

This section was written as of April 2021. In even a few months of this book releasing, this lingo could change, and these words could be terms of the past. However, some of these terms are relatively old, have stuck around, and may be in use for a while. So, learn and use these terms at your discretion.

A lot of these trends and terms come from social media, because most of Gen-Z is constantly on such platforms and is viewing somewhat similar content. This terminology may be very different even a month after this book is published and may not be accurate due to the rapidly changing nature of Gen-Z terminology in tandem with the fast pace of the internet.

Some history and background.

Gen-Z has adopted certain mannerisms and style of speech from AAVE (African American Vernacular English). "AAVE is an established, recognized system of linguistics and a dialect of English natively spoken by Black communities, notably in the United States and Canada." Phrases like "It's the ___ for me," "Chile, anyways," "We been knew," "Finna," "Peri-odt," and "No cap" are rooted in AAVE. Such language has been defined as "internet culture" or "Gen-Z slang," but this is a mislabeling that should be addressed. This is why.[62]

AAVE isn't a product of the twenty-first century. AAVE is influenced by various African languages and has its roots embedded in the institution of slavery in the United States. Historically, AAVE has been looked down upon and seen as "ghetto" or not proper English, yet AAVE has been misused and integrated into the "internet culture machine," produc-ing "trendy" phrases and memes for users' consumption globally. Globalism's extensive role in creating a shared popular culture on the internet contributes to the common misconception that AAVE is internet/Gen-Z/Twitter slang.[63]

The co-opting of AAVE into internet lingo and usage by non-Black people isn't something new or exclusive to Gen-Z as other generations have done the same. But Gen-Z, being a technologically native generation born into the boom of social media and the internet as we know it today, is infamous for its appropriation and misuse of AAVE. Consequently, a majority of the "trendy" words found in Gen-Z's vocabulary are, in fact, AAVE due to the proximity of non-Black people to Black circles and Black communication via Twitter and other social media platforms. [64]

---

62 Zenerations Instagram page, accessed February 10, 2020.
63 Ibid.
64 Ibid.

By reducing a rich, historical, and culturally relevant language to "internet slang," anti-Blackness is perpetuated, whether intended or not, due to the racist, colonial systems that disadvantage and demean Black AAVE speakers. When Black people use AAVE, they are often frowned at or ridiculed for their "bad English" or "bad grammar" by a racist society embedded in oppressive, anti-Black beliefs. [65]

Despite having an established and distinct dialect to communicate, Black people are forced to engage in codeswitching—alternating between two or more languages, or language varieties, in the context of a single conversation—to "fit in" and successfully access the same opportunities as their non-Black counterparts. This language inequity is also influenced by linguistic prescriptivism—the idea that language must adhere to a set of prewritten rules—which is inherently colonialist and racist. [66]

When non-Black people on the internet, specifically Gen-Z, use and misuse AAVE without knowing its origins and attribute it to "internet slang," "stan language," or "meme culture," they are engaging in the commodification of Black culture, which exploits Black people, their language, and means of expression and inventions. Moreover, the short and cyclic life span of AAVE on the internet caused by non-Black people growing tired of certain "internet slang" words and deeming them as cringe or outdated contributes to the degrading of AAVE and its speakers. After the trending AAVE word(s) absorbed and abused by mainstream internet

---

65   Ibid.
66   Ibid.

culture fade away, Black people whose use of the words is linguistic are looked down upon for their continued use of the "dead trend."[676869]

AAVE's short lifespan on the internet and non-Black people's ignorant attitudes of its influence on mainstream "internet slang" was notably seen when famous drag queen Trixie Mattel made a tweet calling for specific phrases rooted in AAVE to be left in 2020. In Black circles, it provoked an ongoing discourse on non-Black and gay people's use/misuse, misunderstanding, and dismissal of AAVE. **Hence, the use of AAVE in non-Black LGBTQ+ circles** is problematized when non-Black gays are ignorant of the origins of some "drag slang/gay-lingo/iconic words" or claim AAVE is meant "for the gays." Staking a claim to AAVE as a non-Black queer person because it is commonly used in LGBTQ+ circles, specifically ball culture and the drag scene, without recognizing Black queer pioneers' influence on the language also contributes to the degradation of AAVE and its native speakers.[7071]

Due to the increasingly interconnected nature of the world, the lines between subculture and mainstream internet culture are blurred as marginalized languages such as AAVE are absorbed and gentrified for everyone's usage. This linguistic gentrification leads to the overwhelming lack of awareness seen

67 Ibid.

68 Arianna Coghill, "The Truth Behind Ebonics," *HerCampus,* January 27, 2017.

69 Imani Benberry, "Dear Non-Black People, AAVE Is Not 'Stan' Or 'Internet Culture," *Study Breaks,* August 24, 2020.

70 @kllingf (Iliana) Twitter Page, accessed February 16, 2020.

71 @brendanrouthRETURNS Reddit page, accessed February 16, 2020.

in non-Black people's unknown use of AAVE, thinking it is "internet slang." It also leads to the demeaning of Black people's use of AAVE offline by the inherently racist perception that it is "improper English" and its speakers are "illiterate," which compels many AAVE speakers to codeswitch.[72][73][74]

Due to the ever-evolving nature of language and popular culture and considering Globalism's role on the internet, it is reasonable to expect that AAVE or any other marginalized language will always be embedded into our "collective lingo." Therefore, the solution to eradicating the collective ignorance and misuse of AAVE and the racist, negative impacts on its Black native speakers is to respect AAVE like any other dialect or language in the world. Like you would do to any language before attempting to use it, learn accurate terminology and research the origins of AAVE. Question if your use or perceptions of AAVE as a non-Black person is embedded in racist, colonial thought and correct any negative implicit biases you may have.[75][76][77][78]

Do not police the use of AAVE by Black speakers or subjugate it to a "trend" with a short lifespan. Speak up when you notice Black people being ridiculed or discriminated against

---

72 Ibid.

73 Zeba Blay, "12 Words Black People Invented, And White People Killed," *The Huffington Post,* August 20, 2015.

74 Eleanor Tremeer, "Is It Cultural Appropriation To Use Drag Slang And AAVE?," *Babbel Magazine,* January 8, 2019.

75 Ibid.

76 Meron Berhe, "AAVE isn't Gen Z slang," *The Pitch, Walter Johnson High School Student Newspaper,* January 4, 2021.

77 Taylor Jones, "What is AAVE?," *Language Jones,* September 19, 2014.

78 Nicole Cardoza, "Respect AAVE.," *Anti-Racism Daily,* July 16, 2020.

for using AAVE. Educate others who are not aware of their use/misuse of AAVE and amplify Black voices.[79][80][81]

So, beyond AAVE... does Black culture manifest anywhere else?

Yes, yes, and yes! These six fashion trends only present some of the countless ways Gen-Z has taken references from Black culture.

- Bucket Hats
    - Originally, bucket hats were designed for farmers and fisherman that would use such hats as protection from the rain. It was then adapted for soldiers, and then as a lady's accessory. However, the bucket hat wasn't seen as a fashion staple until the '80s when Big Bank Hank of the Sugar Hill Gang (a Black rapper) wore one on the TV show *Soap Factory*, and LL Cool J wore a statement red Kangol Bucket Hat.
- Logomania
    - You can't talk about logomania without talking about Dapper Dan, one of the founding fathers of streetwear. Dapper Dan began using fabric enveloped in knockoff designer logos to style popular hip-hop artists, decking covers, curtains, and furniture.
- Oversized clothing
    - The origins of wearing oversized clothing date to '80s hip hop, and stem from Black communities and

79 Ibid.
80 William Brennan, "Julie Washington's Quest to Get Schools to Respect African-American English," *The Atlantic*, April 15, 2018.
81 Lauren Michele Jackson, "We Need to Talk About Digital Blackface in Reaction GIFs," *Teen Vogue*, August 2, 2017.

financial hardship. The improper sizing was due to clothes being handed down from older family members in order to save money. But soon, rappers started performing in baggy clothing to create a casual environment and resonate with audience members.

- Sneaker Culture
  - In 1984, Michael Jordan collaborated with Nike to create the Air Jordan, which revolutionized the sneaker industry. This line of shoes is still popular, and one of Nike's best-selling sneakers, with many companies trying to mimic the colorful design and function of the shoes. Influential Black rappers like Run-DMC and Grandmaster Flash also started to wear sneakers for fashion, which only amplified the comfortable, cool, and trendy image that sneakers were starting to gain, turning a plain item for athleticism and utility into a symbol of wealth and status. Sneakerheads (essentially sneaker fanatics) can tell you that some sneakers are hard to get and run up a large bill as well.

- Scripted Necklaces
  - Such necklaces are ties to culture. These necklaces originated as ways for Black and Brown wearers to proudly show off their "hard to pronounce names" and also were used as ways for communities to indicate that they were responsible enough to own real gold jewelry.
  - If you've watched TV, you've definitely heard of the popular HBO series Sex and the City. In this show, the main character, Carrie Bradshaw (played by Sarah Jessica Parker) has a scripted necklace of her own. But the show perpetuates a whitewashed

narrative which disregards years of criticism Black and Latinx communities faced for wearing flashy jewelry with pride.

- Hoop Earrings
  - POCs have been regarded as unprofessional, ghetto, or ratchet when wearing hoops. There's also a popular saying, "the bigger the hoop, the bigger the hoe." Now yes, this is a bit awry for this book, but it's important to mention. This saying has been used for years to make women in Black and Latinx communities feel ashamed for embracing their culture but is seldom used in regards to white women who are considered trendy and fashionable when they wear hoop earrings. [82]

So, when it comes to Gen-Z trends and language, not all of them are necessarily original. It's poignant to reference the history behind the trends that take inspiration from Black heritage. From bucket hats to the word "bruh," Gen-Z has taken a lot of our "internet culture" from AAVE and Black influences, and we should recognize that.

Emoji Lingo

I didn't include emojis in this section—simply because there are several iterations as to how emojis can be used depending on the situation. For example, the most basic red heart emoji. To most people, this emoji is used to show love, support, or admiration. However, for some, Gen-Zers specifically, the red heart emoji can be used sarcastically, as a passive aggressive

---

82 Zenerations Instagram page, post about Fashion Trends that Originated from Black Culture, accessed February 10, 2020.

way to show dislike/disagreement, or at the end of a sarcastic comment.

So, the same emoji can be used differently in different circumstances, and some emojis can seem like they mean one thing but actually mean another. I'll leave it up to you to look into those cases.

What you've been waiting for:
In alphabetical order for your reference

- ASL- (age, sex, location), (as hell), or (as life); could be used in all three ways, most commonly used "as hell" in conversation "this burrito is good asl"
- BS- Bull S***
- Basic- someone who follows mainstream trends, and doesn't display much individuality; "I don't really have a lot of cool clothes, I'm really basic"
- Beef- to have beef with someone is to have a conflict with someone, or to be holding a grudge against them.
- Bet- a response to a statement, can be used as okay/definitely/for sure "Come with me to the corner store today. Bet."
- Bop/Bops- used to reference a good song or a song that you can vibe to "that song by Cardi B is a bop"
- Bread- referring to cash or money "Let's get this bread," "got to grind to get this bread"
- Bruh- variation of "bro," a filler word that can be used as a response to practically anything "bruh how've you been?" or "that test was hard, bruh"

- bruh girls- girls that aren't really sentimental and aren't basic; they could be described as tomboys, or "one of the boys"
- Bussin- used to describe if something is really good; "this food is bussin!"
- CEO of ___ - someone who does something so many times that they could be the CEO of it; used sarcastically or in a praising manner (used commonly in the comment section of TikTok); "she's the CEO of writing a book;" "She's the CEO of looking good in pictures"
- Clout- having influence, being well known, being successful; can be seen as having fame, power or money; "Beyonce has a lot of clout"
- Cancelled- a reference to cancel culture; when you cancel someone, they have done something to upset you, and in response you are ignoring them; most frequently used lightheartedly
- Can't even- if you "can't even" it means you are upset, irritated, or having a hard time.
- Cap- something that is false; another word for lying; "he's capping... he wasn't at the gym last night; he was at home"
- Chile- pronounced like child but without the d; used when someone does something out of the question; popularized by rapper Nicki Minaj
- Chips- bad/not good; "This day was chips"
- Cloutivism- the notion of doing things for the "clout" or doing something to gain recognition
- Cottagecore- an "aesthetic that revolves around a romanticized life in nature;" motifs like flowers, mushrooms, cottages, flowy clothing, pastel colors, baking, and lattes are associated with cottagecore[83]

---

83 *Urban Dictionary*, s.v. "skinny legend."

- Cut the cameras dead a**- stop what you're doing; hold on
- Drip- Expensive jewelry or clothing; could be used as a word to describe an outfit; "her outfit was drippy"
- Dope- When something is cool; "that shirt is dope"
- E- boy/girl- a boy or girl who has a semi-emo or goth style
- FB: Facebook
- FYP: For You Page
- Echo chamber- "an environment in which a person encounters only beliefs or opinions that coincide with their own, so that their existing views are reinforced, and alternative ideas are not considered."[84]
- Extra- being over the top or excessive; "that girl is so extra, she can't leave anything alone"
- Facts- used to agree with someone/something; "what that YouTuber said in that video was facts"
- Fake- someone who pretends to be something that they're not; "he's so fake, he doesn't really like football"
- Fire- something very cool; "that song is fire"
- For real- abbreviation: fr; used to express agreement with what someone else says; "I have so much work to do... for real"
- Fried- "I can't do this anymore;" or, they're fried on drugs
- Ghosting- ignoring someone you are talking to; "Chris ghosted Grace last week"
- Glooks- (good looks); another way of saying thank you
- Glow up- when someone dramatically improves their appearance
- Go off/went off- hyping someone up; or to go on a rant about a particular subject; "Riya was going off about Gen-Z the other day" or "Riya really went off on her recent on Instagram"

---

84 *Oxford Languages.* s.v. "echo chamber (n.)," accessed Feb 26, 2021.

- Goals- what you aspire to be; "that couple is such goals"
- Goat/Goated- The act of being the (**Greatest of All Time**); "Kobe is such a GOAT for sinking that shot in last night's game"
- Grind/Grinding- when you work really hard/push yourself to achieve something or get something done; could be referencing a work ethic; "I was on my grind last night. I finished three assignments in less than an hour"
- High key- used to describe the actions of someone who did something seriously and aggressively; "she high-key threatened me!" (Is almost never used compared with low-key); "This is high-key annoying"
- Homie- Someone who is your best friend, someone you can always rely on, someone you'll always stand by
- IG: Instagram
- Ice- Expensive jewelry, usually diamonds, popularized by rappers; "Saweetie has so much ice"
- Iconic- something very original or impressive; "her outfit was iconic"
- igh- short form for alright
- Imma- I'm going to; "imma go to the store real quick"
- In my bag- In your feelings, feeling emotional
- It's the ____ for me- term referring to a specific feature/aspect of someone or something; "it's the nice smile for me;" Could be used in a sarcastic/demeaning way
- I'm dead/I'm deceased- when something is so incredibly funny
- KAHDJSJJSKAL- or variations of just typing on keyboard to display excitement; "ashdlfkajhslfh I can't believe I just got that job"
- Karen- A White woman who exhibits racist characteristics

- Like- used in every like, sentence, like, for no specific reason other than just to, like, fill space.
- Lil- short for little; "I'm a lil hungry"
- Lit- Used to describe something amazing.
- Lmao- laughing my a*** off
- Logomania- an article of clothing smothered in a repetitive pattern of a brand's monogrammed logos; often associated with being a symbol of wealth and status
- Lol- laughing out loud
- Love that- popularized by YouTuber James Charles; can be used in a sarcastic tone or when you feel indifferent/don't care about something
- Lowkey- used to describe the actions of someone who did something subtly or as a joke; "She lowkey didn't want to come;" "I lowkey hate this movie"
- Mad- a lot of; "she got mad shoes"
- Mood- when someone does something or expresses an idea or emotion you can relate to; "that's such a mood"
- No cap- don't lie; no lying; "no cap, but this burger is the best one in the country"
- OK Boomer- derogatory term toward the older generation to express irritation with them
- On the Daily- something done on the daily basis, or regularly. Could be used sarcastically where someone is joking about something they should do on the daily but don't; "I work out on the daily"
- Oof- when something unfortunate occurs. Synonymous with ugh; like "rip;" can be used either in reference to oneself or other people; common uses: "That's such an oof," "I didn't do well on that test oof"
- POC- person of color
- POV- point of view

- Period- a word used for emphasis, or another word for facts; usually used after a statement; "the feminist movement needs to be intersectional. Period"
- Prolly- short for probably
- Pull up- come to a place.
- Purr- another word for period; used and popularized by Black LGBT males
- Queen- when someone is incredibly amazing and you aspire to be them, they are a queen
- Recent- a recent post on a social media network; "go like my recent on IG"
- Rip/RIP- used when something goes poorly; when referring to one's own actions, it is synonymous with either "oops" "darn;" when commenting on someone else (I.e. rip John), it employs something bad has happened to that person.
- Rn- (right now); "I can't talk rn"
- Roast- when someone playfully insults someone else, they "roast" them.
- SMH- (shaking my head)
- SC- short form for **S**nap **C**hat
- Snap- referring to Snapchat
- Salty- if someone is mildly upset or irritated with someone or something, they are salty.
- Savage- used to describe someone who does something commendable, brave, or shocking.
- Shook- shocked or surprised, thrown off guard
- Shoot my shot- when you're trying to see if your crush likes you
- Simp- someone that goes out of their way for a crush or someone they like "I'm simping for this girl rn, I bought her everything on her list"

- Sipping tea- listening to gossip
- Skinny legend- A phrase used by a social media sub-group called "stans;" commonly used to refer to celebrities such as Mariah Carey who are glamorous and talented, no matter their weight; also used ironically to refer to cute animals, people, objects etc. Twitter trolls use it often in their memes.[85]
- Slaps- when something is good; "this sandwich slaps"
- Slime- another word for homie/a really cool person
- Spilling tea- sharing gossip
- Stan- (combines the words stalker and fan); an obsessive fan; "I'm a *Mean Girls* stan"
- Sus- short form of suspicious; "that video seems a lil sus"
- TBD- to be determined; "the date of the event is tbd"
- TBH- (to be honest); "tbh I hate the new food in the cafeteria;" "tbh I didn't like that comment on my recent"
- TBT- throwback to; "tbt when we went to that concert"
- That ain't it- when something feels off, or not right
- TTYL- (talk to you later)
- Tea- when someone has juicy gossip or exciting information, they say they have "tea," or that it's "the tea"
- Toxic- used to describe something bad for you, specifically people or technology; "Lisa is so toxic;" "that attitude is so toxic"
- Tweakin- when something/someone doesn't/isn't making sense, is wrong/mistaken, or has done something stupid; "Ashley thinks that the Steelers are the best team out there; she's tweakin"
- U bugging- you're crazy/insane
- U got the whole squad laughing- displaying sarcasm

---

85 *Urban Dictionary*, s.v. "cottagecore (a.)."

- Valid- something that is a fact/makes sense, or someone who is attractive; "she's valid" or "what Riya said the other day was valid"
- W or L- win or loss, but used more colloquially; if something goes well, it's a "dub" or "w" (depending on whether you speak or text, and if something goes poorly it's an "L."
- WTF- what the F***
- Washed- athletes when they're not doing well
- Whip- car
- Woke- politically active/aware; "did you check out that girl's Instagram? She's so woke."
- Word- used as a standalone exclamation, in response to finding out something has gone well; "My teacher moved the essay due date until next Tuesday" "word"
- XD- a laughing face; could replace lol

Chapter 12

Desire to be better-what does that mean and why is that important to us?

—

Madeline Allison of DoSomething.org, Hallie Meyer of Caffe Panna, Nadya Okamato of PERIOD and August, Melissa Kilby of Girl Up, and Lindsay Stein of Campaign Magazine and Bold. I just listed five names that hold immense power in their fields. Madeline, Melissa, and Lindsay are out of Gen-Z. Hallie and Nadya are in it. But each of these people are leading the way to redefining the world for Gen-Z in the future.

Madeline Allison

Madeline, or Maddy, is here for the now, the future, and everything in between. I got to work with Maddy at DoSomething. org, which is a youth-led movement for good. DoSomething. org is both a website and an organization, and it makes it so easy to make change with impact that's actually reasonable. I got to start a district-wide Meatless Mondays program at my high school with DoSomething, register over one hundred and fifty voters as a national voter registration captain, and run fun campaigns like Teens for Jeans as a national club leader, where my school and I donated jeans in collaboration with Aeropostale and DoSomething. Not to mention, DoSomething also has other amazing partnerships with big corporations like College Board, Chevrolet, and Taco Bell.

But enough about me. Although Maddy isn't with DoSomething.org currently, she said that her time there defined her. To Maddy, what keeps DoSomething moving are the youth behind each and every campaign, and the youth feedback that pushes the organization to keep innovating in terms of campaigns, partnerships, and strategy in order to get more actionable change in their communities.

This is the power of Gen-Z. Informing on campaigns that are changing the world one action at a time. People like Maddy take that very Gen-Z messaging and relay that to company executives and organize youth accordingly. And no idea is ever a bad idea.

But for a lot of Gen-Z, making change and speaking up isn't always a choice. Sometimes it's a necessity in order to see change for not only ourselves, but our siblings, community, and future generations. And with the resources we have at our fingertips, it's a no brainer. We have a responsibility to get online and garner support and awareness to the issues that we care about and that have impacted us and those that we know.

Getting out there online is hard. But it's also not. As stated in previous chapters, in a few hours, a local account with a couple hundred followers can have a video with over a million views and likes. This exposure doesn't only inform others on a particular situation, but also creates a global community in which others are aware and invested in the well-being of a particular community.

This is what small actions that stem from organizations like DoSomething garner. Support, awareness, and community, all of which drive Gen-Z to make the impossible, possible.

Hallie Meyer

Hallie Meyer is a chef and a business owner. Hallie owns Caffe Panna, a cafe with a star drink of her take on a classic affogato (which is ice cream with espresso). Now in a chapter full of fashion, why food?

Food is a way that we can communicate, a medium for our stories, cultures, and traditions, and really, food is just really good. Hallie's journey is really interesting, and how she developed her idea for Caffe Panna makes the scoop even more worthwhile.

Hallie started as someone who wanted to do service and give back to her community. Hallie ended up working with a school, where she was with students in an after-school cooking club. And in a school cafeteria, you really don't have a kitchen. You barely have any cooking utensils, maybe some cutting boards. And so, to Hallie, ice cream was the perfect thing to bring where she and the kids she was with could talk about what was happening before their eyes, and students really loved it.

That's where Hallie saw the power of ice cream. After finishing her year of service with AmeriCorps, Hallie then moved to Italy to work in a gelateria to crystalize her concept.

So Caffe Panna came about for Hallie. Not only was it an ode to her love of the gelato and espresso culture of Italy, but as Hallie puts it, "ice cream is such a bridge builder. All you have to do is say, 'Hey, I have an ice cream store. Like, hey, come visit my ice cream and coffee shop.' Those are the most universally joyful things ever." From there, Hallie and her team at Caffe Panna developed a menu with different flavors, ranging from a traditional stracciatella to a blueberry birthday cake.

So, why ice cream?

To Hallie, ice cream was a cool opportunity because you can talk to anyone about ice cream. You can ask questions like what's your favorite flavor? What do you want to make today? "It's like a really cool blank canvas, which is especially empowering."

But how does this relate to Gen-Z?

Gen-Z wants to see something new. We want food that we can post on our Instagram stories and aesthetically pleasing plates that will make our social media feeds. I've gone to restaurants that didn't even have that great-tasting food, but the food was "Instagrammable" regardless.

So back to Hallie. Hallie's cafe has five specials that rotate weekly. That's five different ice cream flavors per week. So, for Hallie's cafe, the ice cream never stays the same, and that's what gets people coming back through her door. For a lot of people, as Hallie described, it's a "Pokémon strategy" where "you've got to catch them all." (Pokémon strategy is referring to the Pokémon card game where the more cards you have, the better).

Hallie is also able to play on people's interest in nontraditional combinations, especially Gen-Zers. (We love non-traditional combinations when it comes to food. Take Tony Baloney's famous pizza restaurant with combinations like ramen pizza and taco pizza, which I can attest to are very good.) When it comes to Gen-Z, the narrative that we portray is about what you support, and where you eat. Where you eat says something about who you are, where previously, a meal was just a meal.

Not to mention, Hallie channels authenticity through her work every day. When I asked her about how her cafe will sustain itself through social media trends, Hallie quoted Stephen Sondheim, who said "anything you do, let it come from you, then it will be new." To Hallie, authenticity means only creating what you want to create. And if you can stick with that, then it will always be fresh and true.

But beyond ice cream, Hallie also learned two things from her time working with students.
- The food inequality problem
- Exposure to different foods and cultures for young people

She said that food inequality is a big problem in the United States, but also in the world. Food inequality has several intersections, from people not receiving nutritional food, to not having food at all, and even parts of communities that have food deserts, which are "geographic areas where access to affordable, healthy food options (aka fresh fruits and veggies) is limited or nonexistent because grocery stores are too far away."[86]

Hallie also mentioned how powerful of a tool food was in conveying culture and history. It exposed students to new flavors, tastes, and experiences, from the very same kitchen they were making ice cream in. Food is also a reminder of the reasons that everyone's own cultures and traditions are important, which serves as a tool for empowerment and upliftment. To Hallie, ice cream wasn't the most important thing that she got to facilitate in the kitchen, but rather when a student brought their own their own home recipe or said, "Hey, this is what my grandma makes for us."

These individuals each bring their own stories and passions into the work that they do every single day. From shoes to ice cream, Gen-Z is diverse, not only in terms of ethnicity, but in thought, and what we're doing for a living. For Gen-Zers, chasing your dreams *is a viable possibility*. It's not something you chalk up to naïveté fifty years later. We're able to integrate our integral values within our businesses and move forward in a society where we can be who and what we want to be.

---

86 United States Department of Agriculture Economic Research Service, "Access to Affordable and Nutritious Food: Measuring and Understanding Food Deserts and Their Consequences."

Nadya Okamoto

Period. A word that could mean many things to many people, but Nadya Okamoto has turned this word into a social movement striving for equity in the menstrual space. Nadya started the organization when she was just sixteen years old and has continued to be a fierce advocate for the cause. Okamoto said that "It's exciting to see other young people innovating and mobilizing in this movement to end period poverty and stigma."

But wait, periods. As of now, menstruation is still a pretty taboo topic. But Gen-Z is willing to talk about sex, sexuality, sex education, periods, and even more. Really, we're open to it all because we want to destigmatize these conversations that can potentially lead to problems later on. We're more comfortable with our sexuality as well, which intersects with the conversation around periods, because not all women are menstruators, and not all menstruators are women.

Nadya said that she "grew up being the kid in the class group project who wanted to do it all myself to get it done faster and to my standards, but, when growing an organization, I had to learn that a good leader is one who brings on and empowers other leaders." She talked about the importance of a team and the fact that the work behind the scenes of large social movements is hard, and that one cannot "do it alone," so "it's important to build a team and delegate work!"

Specifically in the menstrual space, "The stigma surrounding periods has always been a barrier because it's not just a 'women's issue;' this is a human issue, and it affects us all. It is 2021, and yet, thirty US states still have a sales tax on period products because they are considered non-essential items (unlike Rogaine and Viagra), period-related pain is a leading cause of absenteeism amongst girls in school, and too many menstruators don't have access to the period products they need."

The fact that there is little to no education surrounding issues like sales tax on period products or even the menstrual cycle in general in our education systems makes it harder to advocate for, and harder to get people of all ages and genders on board with the issue as well. This is where Gen-Z comes into play, being the best advocates and activists for such social issues, and to be that bridge between other generations such as Gen-X, Boomers, and Millennials. This goes to show the importance of intersectionality in any social movement, and Okamoto says that "People should be valued for their whole selves and holistically supported in all aspects of their identity—including around periods."

On the topic of bridging generations, Nadya mentioned that she was "very fortunate that I've been able to turn my passion into my profession and I owe that, in part, to mentors I've had. Older generations can support young people by sharing opportunities, uplifting their voices, and offering mentorship if they are able!" Nadya has a point in this because each generation has their own skillsets and value. Boomers and Gen-Xers may have more office and in-person work experience that can help with areas such as Human Relations, or working on a team, where Gen-Zers could have more technological skills. Playing off of each generation's strengths will really help us come together as a society and destigmatize intergenerational conversation.

According to Okamoto, who acknowledged that she has a more progressive take on all of the questions that I asked her, said that social media, sustainability, racial justice, and gender inclusivity were issues that she felt particularly resonated with the Gen-Z generation. Social media is clearly something that defines Gen-Z as a generation, and around 73 percent of Gen-Z utilizes social platforms. Okamoto mentions how "Social media is an amazing tool to reach Gen-Z."[87]

She said how she used her "social media presence to talk about period poverty, normalize menstruation and fight the period stigma, share her life and be vulnerable about what she has been through or is dealing with, and galvanize her community to join her in fighting for systemic change." This allows her to really connect and interact with her audience, but also develop a community of people that agree with her views, values, and issues that she is an advocate for, such as the menstrual movement.

Nadya mentions how in her work with PERIOD, she was "really focused on building a platform for young people to feel empowered to make change in their community through PERIOD's chapter network which is youth-led." PERIOD's chapter network is one of the reasons that they are so successful. Chapter leaders are able to advance work in the menstrual space through the lens of their own community and are able to tailor content to suit their audience the best.

---

87 "Why Do Different Generation Use Social Media?" *Marketing Charts*, October 21, 2019.

Nadya stepped away from PERIOD as executive director in January 2020 to start her new company, August (itsaugust.co). August is a lifestyle period brand working to reimagine period care to be powerful. Products will be launching late Spring 2021.

Nadya says that she always strives to listen to the community and their needs; she also knows it's a learning process. Nadya is currently all focused with her new start-up, August, and with a product launch. Her future goals build on her experiences with her past at PERIOD.

In general, Nadya says that Gen-Z "taps into the power of social media for community building and social justice. We love to engage and collaborate with people across the world that we've never met but still consider friends. For us, social media isn't just a tool, it's a part of our life and often an integral part of our self-expression."

Nadya says that what sets Gen-Z apart from other generations is "A heightened sense of individual responsibility to mobilize and try to make this world a better place—whether that be organizing for justice, bringing joy to people with social content, or simply being a kind and understanding person. I also think that Gen Z has a sort of 'fed-up' attitude and are not going to sit around waiting for people to give them permission to work or organize—they're ready. They're young. And together, they are unstoppable."

Funny enough, I met Nadya at an event for Girl Up, whose executive director is Melissa Kilby, and my next interview. I was a teen advisor for Girl Up, so I got to work closely with

Melissa and the staff at Girl Up. The reason I bring this up is because I know that Girl Up is led by youth like myself to make gender equality a reality.

Melissa Kilby

When I talked to Melissa, she said, "The way to make change is all about prioritizing. And I prioritize youth." I couldn't agree with Melissa more. Girl Up follows a club model led by girls similar to the chapter model of PERIOD.

When I asked Melissa why youth cares about being better, she said "you're expected to be better, and you put those expectations on yourselves." But Melissa isn't wrong there. With social media, and with the internet, comparing yourself with other people is easy. Most of the times, this manifests as imposter syndrome. But, as Theodore Roosevelt said, "Comparison is the thief of joy." So, setting the bar too high for ourselves and for our generation creates the pressure to be perfect—even though perfection means something different to every person, and even though perfection isn't what one should strive for.

A lot of the Girl Up leaders who lead clubs internationally are also activists. And there's a power in being a **youth** activist. Not only are you able to call attention to world leaders without, say, losing your job, or having anything on the line, you're also able to navigate social networks better in order to make your activism more efficient and effective, where your message could reach more people, more quickly, and bring attention to the issue(s) that you're advocating for.

There's a small window for being a youth, and a Gen-Zer, but it's a powerful one, one that we can use to our advantage. In the little time that Gen-Z has really even been alive, we've made colossal strides. Let's even look at the United States 2020 election. The election was between Joe Biden and Donald Trump. I'd argue that youth turned out to vote if they could and did a lot of the behind-the-scenes work, which resulted in an election with record voter turnout and more people engaged in issues that affected the country than ever before. We also called out President Trump online, from Twitter to Instagram, and weren't even slightly afraid to do so.

We're not only able to make change because we have more resources but because we want to do better. As Melissa said, "our communities aren't just the white, Christian neighborhoods that we once had. Now we have immigrant communities, and more diverse communities." To some people this might seem like a bad thing. But diversity is a big factor as to why Gen-Z is able to think outside the box and come up with innovative solutions because we've been exposed to various perspectives from day one. And the people in our neighborhoods and communities only provide one set of perspectives. Social media provides another set of perspectives that can expand our own.

Let's take a deeper dive into diversity for a quick second. For example, we're all looking at a painting. One of those really confusing ones, where anyone could take anything from the image. I might think I see people walking to a vast ocean, where another friend could think this same image is actually fish outside the water, representing the effects of climate change. These two narratives couldn't be more far apart, but we both got these ideas from looking at the same image. This is the power of diversity—being able to see the same thing from different perspectives. And so, in a broader context, this applies outside of just paintings, this applies to political concepts, world issues, and business. Diversity can help us create innovative solutions that can power change in the future, and that is why diversity is an essential characteristic of Gen-Z.

In terms of equality, we can think about all of the identities that we bring to equality. Our individual identities and the things that make us unique should not be the things that make us unequal, but rather those that bring us together as a community. Melissa says that "this generation will actually start to bring us back together as a community. The openness to each other, to differences, and the acceptance of each other is so dire and needed in the world right now."

This is all great, but there's also a bit of not so great. We have a burning desire to make change. It's almost innate for Gen-Z. But sometimes, even the most genuine of activism can be seen as performative because you almost have this need to post or else your image in the eyes of other people goes down and doesn't seem as genuine anymore. We almost have to be aware of every single thing that is going on in the world as Gen-Zers if we want to speak up. Because we have twenty-four-hour news where as soon as something happens it will be reported on. We have everything accessible, so there's no excuse not to post about something going on in the world. **Our efforts have to move as fast as the internet does, or we'll be left behind because of it.**

But this desire for change and to be better isn't just present in the activist community. It's also something that pops up almost everywhere and anywhere. Even on TikTok, Gen-Z is talking about manifesting their best life, and working hard to achieve their dreams, whatever they might be. There are even videos about how to do certain things or break into certain careers like from affiliate marketing to medical school.

However, I have to talk about burnout. Burnout is especially present in Gen-Z because it's always a "go, go, go" attitude with Gen-Z. Sometimes it feels like there's no stopping. If you have a certain personality on Instagram for example, whether that be an activist that informs their community or even an influencer that is posting brand deals, you have to be posting probably a couple times a week, which includes posting on the feed, on Instagram stories, and possibly on Instagram TV or Reels. And that's just Instagram. Sometimes, it's really hard to keep up this persona and engage with the people that follow you because there's an understanding that once you put something out there, and really put yourself out there, there's no turning back.

You have to think about optics, and what would look good to post when—an Instagram aesthetic—and even consider looking at your Instagram analytics (only available if your account is public) where Instagram tells you when the best time is to post for optimal interaction, and tells you what kind of content gets the most interactions on your feed.

But, back to burnout. "'Today's world may be a more competitive and less forgiving place, but when that assessment yields a constricted definition of personal success, it fans the flames of destructive perfectionism. It's vital to recall how varied the pathways are to a happy and successful life,' to break from all-or-nothing thinking, and to develop the ability to accept disappointments and challenges without falling apart."[88] There's also so much opportunity out there, with a career space that is broadening day by day. So, Gen-Zers are almost constantly being bombarded with everything that is available.

And although "Gen-Z is most likely to report poor mental health and seek help,"[89] that doesn't mean that they don't deal with issues like burnout by themselves. "Burnout reduces productivity and saps your energy, leaving you feeling increasingly helpless, hopeless, cynical, and resentful. Eventually, you may feel like you have nothing more to give. The negative effects of burnout spill over into every area of life—including your home, work, and social life."[90]

So you can see why this is a problem.

Lindsay Stein

With a desire to be better, what does the future of journalism look like?

This is where I talked to Lindsay Stein, the current CEO of Today, I'm Brave, the former editor at Campaign US, and a

---

88 MaryKate Wust, "How Gen Z Can Swap Burnout for Break-throughs," *Penn Medicine News,* March 21, 2019.

89 American Psychological Association, "Stress in America, Generation Z," October 2018.

90 "Burnout Prevention and Treatment," *HelpGuide,* October 2020.

reporter at AdAge and PR Week. Essentially, Lindsay is more than qualified to talk about this.

But let's get to it. When I talked to Lindsay, she said that right now, journalism is a mix of storytelling, public speaking, and sharing really important stories of people that wouldn't typically make the news because those narratives are important and people want to see them. So now, we're seeing a focus on real and authentic storylines instead of clickbait, in addition to breaking out of the traditionally white space of journalism to more diversity, from the reporters to the people that stories are about.

However, this can be hard. Algorithms aren't exclusive on social media, but are also present on news websites, and more. The fact of the matter is that algorithms are paid for, and sometimes they're targeted really well. So even though we're in this space of creating real and authentic stories, it is still very reasonable to be trapped in your own echo chamber.

However, in the name of storytelling, there can be an oversaturation of storytelling with too much opinion in the news, and sometimes not enough objective facts. And this can lead to distrust in the media, which means a need for more accountability in the journalism space.

But to journalists, editors, and people in the journalism space, beyond having diversity, and beyond having more authentic news is caring about the ROI or return on investment. "ROI is a key performance indicator (KPI) that's often used by

businesses to determine profitability of an expenditure."[91] In media, "you take the sales growth from that business or product line, subtract the marketing costs, and then divide by the marketing cost. So, if sales grew by $1,000 and the marketing campaign cost $100, then the simple ROI is 900 percent."[92]

So now we know that ROI is important, and the revenue can be generated by ads, which is why ad placement via algorithms has brought companies a lot of money. In the future however, we can look for strategic ad placement, and a push for campaigns that represent what our world looks like and who Gen-Z is and who Gen-Z wants to be, pushing forward our desire for social good, and to create around the notion of being better.

Overall, Gen-Z wants to be better, whether that be through simple actions in their own communities, or leading and catalyzing around issues that they are passionate about. Gen-Z is able to use the resources that we have to create this change, but at a cost—with the world moving a little faster every single day. So, is making change hard? Totally. But Gen-Z does it anyway, because we want to be better.

91 Erica Hawkins, "Importance of ROI: Why it matters for all businesses," *Call Rail.*

92 Andrew Beattie, "How to Calculate the Return on Investment (ROI) of a Marketing Campaign," Updated March 2, 2020.

Chapter 13

Collective trauma, and bridging generations

———

Trauma. According to Merriam Webster dictionary, trauma can be defined as "a disordered psychic or behavioral state resulting from severe mental or emotional stress or physical injury."[93]Add collective to the front of that definition, and you can piece together that Gen-Z, collectively, is different as a generation in terms of behavior and thinking due to all of the trauma that we've experienced.

From being born after or a few years before 9/11, growing up through the 2008 financial crisis, and seeing school shootings and injustices through our mobile devices, we've been through a lot at a young age. Not to mention, doing school or working for the first time in a global pandemic. This is what collective trauma is, the weight of which Gen-Z is carrying, and will be carrying into the future.

---

93   s.v. "trauma"

Dylan Miars

Professor Dylan Miars is the youngest paid instructor in the United States, teaching on the UC Berkeley Campus. He facilitates a coursework within the ethnic studies department dedicated to stress management, emotional well-being, and underrepresented groups.

Miars works to educate the Berkeley student population on what it means to be a minority and talks about what it means to experience stress. He answers questions like: What does it mean to be a minority? What types of minorities are there? How do we define privilege?

What makes Miars's class unique is the discussion of minorities extends beyond racial minorities and into cultural minorities, religious minorities, sexual and gender minorities, and the implications that has in one's development and one's ability to be an active citizen in today's world.

Now, you could be asking, how is this relevant to anything in this book? Professor Miars's class goes to show the importance of learning about diversity, and how this has a place at one of the most prestigious universities in the world. Miars also does some interesting research on the genetics of trauma. This research will truly blow your mind; he studies how trauma and mental illness are passed down through generations through your DNA. This field is called epigenetics.

But what exactly does epigenetics mean? Epigenetics deals with DNA methylation, where certain genes are more expressed than others due to the lifestyle choices of our ancestors.

For example, if one's mother was a smoker, certain genes in your DNA would be less or more expressed due to her lifestyle choice. However, Miars's research shows that DNA can be methylated not only through lifestyle choices, but trauma as well. Those who have been through traumatic events or have histories of depression, anxiety, and other mental trauma can pass this on to future generations.

Here's another example. Bob, for instance, has had a regular childhood. However, Bob's father's father, or Bob's grandfather, was a raging alcoholic. This of course doesn't quite affect Bob as much as it did Bob's dad. But Bob's dad's neurotransmitters and resiliency were affected, which deterred the formation of coping mechanisms in terms of alcohol for Bob's dad. This would lead Bob's dad's DNA to methylate (which controls gene expression) and would lead key replicating factors in Bob's dad's DNA exposed to mutation. Now, where does Bob come into play, and why is this relevant to his life? Although Bob had a great childhood, he might end up with alcoholism issues down the line or bad hangovers to the extent where Bob can't consume alcohol.

Now, you might be a little lost. And believe me, if I didn't take a grueling year of Advanced Placement Biology (shoutout to my bio teacher for putting up with me, by the way) I would be too. But the point here is that typically, we view genetics as an idea of nature. However, we need to explore the nurture side of genetics and how the choices that we take in our daily lives can have an effect on those around us, and even our relatives in the future. I won't bore you with the science of all of this, but if you're interested, check out the Yehuda studies, by Dr. Rachel Yehuda of Mount Sinai.

Back to how this point is relevant though. When you look at a generation like Gen-Z, that is the youngest generation so far, many scoff when people say that the generation has "been through a lot." This is a mixture of a lack of awareness of what this group has actually gone through and the effect that that's had.

While this generation is the youngest, we've already experienced two financial crashes, and we're living through a global pandemic. If you were born in the year 2001 or later in the United States, you only ever lived in a world where the US has been at war with some country.

Gen-Z has been born in the midst of the most radical shift in normal, day-to-day activities—which form new collective traumas. And what makes this worse? We can't develop good coping mechanisms and are left with general adaptation syndrome (GAS). "GAS is the three-stage process that describes the physiological changes the body goes through when under stress." The three stages include the alarm reaction stage, the resistance stage, and the exhaustion stage. And what makes GAS worse is that it not only affects Gen-Zers mentally, but also physically, leading to increases in stress hormones and a weakened immune system.

And so, not only did we experience these traumas (and are currently experiencing them), but these very traumas are occurring during our most formative years. We are also able to share injustices that we might have been blind to prior to the internet. Point being, we are living through collective traumas as a generation.

Miars said while analyzing the mental health of Gen-Z, he's noticed the mental health numbers increasing in Gen-Z are in part due to an increased awareness.

This is the same idea as whenever one discovers a new physical element. When we became more aware of cancer, we suddenly saw a massive number of people with that particular spike of cancer dying. Now we're aware of it. Mental health issues have always been around, and older generations are not breaking the cycle of trauma, so this very cycle is being passed down to their children, and we're becoming more aware.

> *"Often times people from earlier generations will say that we invent an illness at some point like ADHD or depression and suddenly the numbers rise. That's not true at all. It has always existed; we just finally gave such illnesses a name and gave recognition to the problem. Gen Z's growing mental illness problem is due not only to our collective trauma, but because of our heightened awareness. So, while heightened awareness doesn't mean more problems necessarily, it means that we are finally able to treat the problems that have been covert for so long."*
>
> —DYLAN MIARS

Another reason why Gen-Zers are so sad? It's simple. We're essentially being given shots of dopamine through our devices and time on social media. And when we sign off from those very devices, we're left wanting more.

One of the hardest traits for Gen-Z to embody is that of compassion and empathy, because that's something we think is so easy to do. We share our mental health post on Facebook or on Instagram, but we can't really empathize with others going through such circumstances because we can barely deal with our own.

And while we've also seen a great surge in liberalism and a great increase in human rights that our generation is privy to, causing and benefiting from, we're also seeing democracy almost hanging by a thread. We're seeing a rise in strongman politics. The Cold War was supposed to be a definitive triumph of democracy but right now, we are seeing firsthand the collapse of such.

Bridging Generations—conversations with...
Lesley Jane Seymour

There is still so much valuable information and valuable things we need to do. As Gen-Zers, we can't abandon generations beyond our parents' generation (Gen-Xers) and Boomers, and those that are older than Gen-Xers can't abandon younger generations like Gen-Z either.

For Gen-Zers, sometimes, we have to understand that past generations were living in a different world. Certainly, there are things that have never been okay throughout time and cannot be excused. However, this doesn't mean that we can totally ignore their lived experiences, the lessons that they've learned, or deem that older generations don't deserve compassion and room for growth. If we can facilitate this sort of "give or take" when it comes to understanding those from generations out of our own, we can rebuild the bridge to other generations, where we can grow society together.

On the topic of bridging generations, I got to talk to Lesley Jane Seymour, an American editor, author, and entrepreneur. She was previously a senior editor of *Vogue* and editor-in-chief of many women's magazines, including *YM, Marie Claire*, and *Redbook*. As someone that is not part of Gen-Z, Seymour offered some intriguing insights to the state of Gen-Z and how our generation is different from those that came before us, but also similar at the same time.

Seymour started off our interview with the statement "I love Gen-Z!" She went on to say that she thinks that Gen-Z is really very close in values to Boomers and Gen-Xers.

She said, "I feel like they absorb a lot of our caring about the world, a lot of our activism that might have skipped over the Millennials." Lesley is a parent, and she said that "Millennials were kind of a reaction," and that "Millennials were raised to be the opposite of the way that we were raised. We had all these very authoritarian parents from the fifties. And so, we wanted to be the opposite. So, we raised them that way. And so, they're a little babyish, where Gen-Z is tougher."

Lesley said, "There's no point in fighting each other. We each have different skill sets and when you put those two skills sets together. It's magical. You've got a skill set with experience and you've got a skill set that knows how to do modern technology." All we need to do is come together and find equity in opportunity moving forward in the future.

A solution is cross mentoring. You have younger people mentor older people and technology, and you have older people mentoring younger people in business savvy, how to handle themselves, how to stick to it when things don't go their way, and how to manage.

Gen-Z is almost forced to grow up earlier, because things like cancel culture and things from their most formative years can come up and be a red flag in their next job interview, or a run for political office. As you grow up, you change, and in our new world, there needs to be a way in which you can edit your profile. When people first go on to social media, they follow trends and are naive. The case is extremely different say five years later, but what that particular individual has done in those five years cannot be erased, because everything on the internet is permanent. While people look through public records and documents to find dirt on people currently, it's going to be much easier to just look at someone's Facebook or Instagram and do investigating that way.

According to Lesley, "Gen-Z is living life for the pictures versus living life for the experience." I'd agree to disagree. Although this might be true, our lives are online, and sharing our experiences is our life to an extent. You could find ways to disagree and agree, but it's a valid point of debate, nonetheless.

I digress, but the social media algorithms create a bubble. Politically, this is extremely dangerous. If you're being fed images and ideas that make you happy, you're subject to confirmation bias. As social media, I'm never going to introduce you to something you don't already like, because that makes you click more and that makes me sell more ads. "Networks have no interest in doing anything but feeding your happiness," according to Lesley. "We need to learn how to get ourselves out of these algorithms that feed us sugar every time we hit the like button and broaden our perspectives. Sometimes you need to eat your brussels sprouts and understand they're good for you, and they make you a better person."

It's hard for you to be your own editor, because you don't know enough. So, you need to be exposed to new things, you need to try new things, and you need to taste new things. You need to know if you're not the type of person to force yourself out there to listen to things you think you don't like, to try new things you may think are yucky.

There used to be a lack of communication, but now we have so much communication we don't know what to believe. Everybody's overcommunicating. I think there should be a course taught in college and taught in high school about digital safety, how to know what's real, and how to be a critical thinker.

For me, my parents have had several different experiences than I have had. They grew up without technology, so for them certain things are important. For example, if we go on vacation, for them it might be looking at the scenery and looking at the view, but for me it might be getting the best picture just to show that I was there; and those small nuances set us apart. Those different experiences define us and set us apart. They can be helpful too. Some things that my parents say are helpful to me, but I can teach them other things.

However, when it comes to the child teaching the parent, most parents aren't always as open. I know that from my own experience. When my parents teach me something, it's natural. It's a parent's job to teach their kid. However, if the roles are switched, it can be uncomfortable, for both parties. As a generation, we have more information for a particular topic, which is always something to consider. We have so many more resources that I don't think other generations really consider, and we are exposed to numerous viewpoints.

My parents couldn't necessarily voice their opinions at their jobs, but if I was uncomfortable with something in my workplace I would go straight to social media and could start a movement against such injustices. That's the kind of power that we have, and sometimes we don't always realize that we have this very power. I think that other generations are starting to pick up on it and are even a bit intimidated by this. We have the potential to be successful younger. There are children coding apps at ten or fifteen years old, becoming millionaires, where usually this sort of wealth was preserved for legacies or people over the age of sixty. This in and of itself is a large generation gap.

and Anna Blue!

I was interested in the topic of intergenerational unity and wanted to hear from someone from Gen-X, Gen-Z's parent's generation. I got to talk to Anna Blue, the Next Gen director at the Female Quotient and former co-director at Girl Up. Anna is essentially leading a new segment of business, about advancing women and advancing equality in the workplace, but focusing on certain aspects of this large topic. She poses questions like, how do we build a more equitable pipeline? How do we build more equitable opportunities, so that young women don't get a job and then look to leave after the first two years because they realize all the barriers for them?

Anna gets to tackle equality in the workplace, and at the entry level. This is different than others, because a lot of the conversations are around middle management, and not enough around the entry level. She says that if you lose people in the first couple of years, you won't have them, period.

Anna says that "sadly, some of the divide isn't, isn't because of us, right? The divide is men tend to hire people and promote people who look like them, who they can relate to, in some way, who they built a relationship with on the golf course, or they love the same football team. And it's a hard space sometimes for women and young people to infiltrate. A lot of times what gets focused on is how do we fix it? How do we show women how to lean in? How do we show women how to speak up? How do we tell women how to advocate for themselves, but it shouldn't be our responsibility to make things equal, we're not the ones holding the power." Recognizing this is essential for equity and ensures that we don't make false assumptions as we go through the workplace.

Anna spoke about one of her biggest challenges, which is with the higher education system. She feels as though it doesn't actually prepare young people for what careers exist. Anna says that "there is nothing that I could have majored in, in college that would have prepared me to lead a nonprofit to go out there and raise money, to understand a whole new generation. I think we need to better prepare young people with an actual understanding of career paths, first and foremost, because then it won't really matter who's standing behind you, who's supporting you, who's in your corner, because you'll feel like you have that direction."

Another highlight from Anna's interview was this quote: "one of the first barriers to equality in the workplace is that all of us go in thinking, we're going to be the exception. Gen-Z knows that women do not get paid the same as men. We know the issues surrounding mental health in the workplace, and the huge level of anxiety and stress, but nobody deals with it." Gen-Z almost creates its own barriers with the notion of knowledge is power. Which it is, but at the same time, we still convince ourselves that we are not the exception, when chances are, that's not true.

"So instead of coming in and saying, I'm going to get to the bottom of this, and I'm going to advocate for it, and I'm going to work for it, and I'm going to point out where those missteps are, and the misguided ways that my company has set up structures, you sort of just become part of the problem, because you convince yourself that you're not part of the problem, if that makes sense, right."

"So I would say that for young women, especially, and especially the most marginalized groups, young women of color, young women with disabilities in the LGBTQ+ community, understand that you are not the exception. You are most likely not the exception, own that. So that way you can start much earlier in finding who your tribe is, and who are the affinity groups that have been able to challenge the status quo, because you don't want to get to middle management and realize that you've been paid $20,000 less all along.

Understand that you are not the exception. And that's okay, because knowledge is power."

"So I would say before you use social media as a tool for your advocacy against the place that signs your checks, I understand if there are other ways that you can be an advocate that might actually work better. I think it's really easy for Gen-Z to automatically go to social media to sort of air out all of your grievances. And in a lot of cases, that's fine. But when you work there, if it is a place that you want to see make a change, but you're committed to being there alongside them, then that might not be the best way. Then I would say, there's so many ways to be an activist, and to be an advocate for something and social media doesn't always have to be your go to."

If you are at a place like Facebook, and there's something that you don't like happening, is there something else that you can do internally? Is there a town hall you can help organize? Is there a petition you can help organize? Can you actually do it in a powerful and significant way internally, before turning your external voice on? And I think that's overall something that's really important for Gen-Z to learn. There is activism beyond protesting and social media. There's a whole spectrum of advocacy and activism in the middle of that, that sometimes your generation loses sight of. You either show up on the front line, which has its place, and is very powerful, or you're a keyboard warrior, which also has its place and is powerful. But there's also a lot of grey area between those two extremes that Gen-Z can explore.

Currently, we can think about the generational dilemma like large buckets, with each generation having their own bucket. What's wrong about that analogy though is that there is no overlap or intersection amongst the generations, which isn't productive in a society. We've started to become more polarized, where it's generation versus generation, when that shouldn't be the case whatsoever. It shouldn't be one generation versus everyone else, but rather generations working together to solve problems that are facing our society.

To me, Lesley and Anna's perspective on Gen-Z was inspiring and fresh. Not a lot of people outside of Gen-Z think like they do. But this just goes to show how much needs to change—in our attitudes, our thinking, and our perception of Gen-Z—in order to move forward.

Mental health

Gen-Z comes into life and experiences with so much knowledge and information and having technology as a resource since birth. Gen-Z has witnessed a lot in a really short amount of time. At a young age, members of Gen-Z have seen people get shot. And even though this is secondhand, it is equally as traumatic. Our generation carries this collective trauma and is impacted because of it, to the point where it doesn't matter if I lived in a really privileged neighborhood with no crime rate because I still have this technology that can give me this experience. This can be good but also bad because that contributes to the mental health issues that define our generation. Equating seeing violence via technology (on phones, TV, etc.) with actually witnessing violence feels insensitive, especially with the explicit mention of living in a privileged neighborhood.

But what I'm trying to say is that technology today allows for more people to view violence that has been recorded, which therefore leads to more people potentially being traumatized having seen such events, and essentially having to face the fact that violence is happening, and that other teens are experiencing such events firsthand.

Experiencing violence can manifest differently for everyone. After hearing, reading, and seeing video about the tragic asphyxiation of George Floyd by white police officers, and not seeing much justice being given for George Floyd, and other victims of racial injustice and violence, I personally was taken aback. Living in a diverse community, being a person of color (POC) and knowing that this is something that is happening to people around the country and is a reality for people was heartbreaking. I needed to take a few days off social media because I was just so heartbroken.

However, some of my peers were able to act right away and organized protests in my town and other towns nearby. However, we all bear this collective trauma because although the way that myself and my peers processed this information and series of events was different, we still saw the same video, and experienced the unrest that resulted.

Additionally, with technology there's just so much information out there that it gets kind of overwhelming at times, and it becomes really hard to strike a balance, which is what Gen-Z struggles with a lot. Gen-Z struggles with understanding our limits. Personally, I always have a million things open, a million things to do, and a million emails to write. All of this pending work seems to never get done and no matter what I do, never seems to be enough, which then goes into the imposter syndrome that our generation faces as well with all of these expectations coming from so many different places.

Just writing this, I feel overwhelmed, and that's really hard on a teenager and young adult, having to manage all of this with school, possibly a job, and in these occupations. Gen-Z is pressured to do well, whether that be being valedictorian, or taking an insane amount of AP courses, or even getting a more career-oriented job that can score points on a college resume.

There's always something to do in our generation, and this contributes to how overwhelmed and stressed our generation is. There's this perpetual "go" button without any brakes and no stopping in between which just becomes tiring. It's hard to establish these limits and even control oneself. I could be scrolling through TikTok for hours and not even understand that so much time has gone by, and this is almost justified with "needing a break" where this indulging behavior only perpetuates the problem further.

Not having this willpower to stop, and not knowing when to stop is another large reason why the mental health of Gen-Z is so impacted. Gen-Z can get sucked into things and get overwhelmed easily. We have grown up with social media, and being so young, it's hard to set limits and not get addicted. Need some evidence? Here are ten statistics that show the extent to which Gen-Z, and really the world, is being impacted by social media.

- 3.1 billion people are social media users worldwide (that's about one-third of the world's population)

- Two hundred and ten million people are estimated to suffer from internet and social media addictions (this one speaks for itself)
- Seventy-one percent of people sleep with or next to their mobile phone. (Social media addiction doesn't just affect behavior during the day; it even damages people's ability to sleep. Some 47 million people in America do not get enough sleep, and 55 percent more teens were sleep deprived in 2015 than in 1991. Exposure to screens before bed is a large factor in exacerbating sleep disorders; 35 percent of people using phones less than average experienced sleep difficulty compared to 42 percent of those with average or above average phone usage.)
- The average person spends more time in front of electronic devices than asleep daily, at eight hours and forty-one minutes.
- Over 240 million Americans check Facebook daily (that's 74 percent of all Americans)
- Ten percent of teens check their phones more than ten times per night. (If prolonged exposure to screens wasn't bad enough for people's sleep, social media addictions are making it even harder for people to get a good night's sleep. Forty-five percent of people check social media instead of sleeping, and roughly 10 percent of teens check their phones more than ten times per night.)
- Teens who spend five hours a day on their phones are two times more likely to show depressive symptoms
- Young, single females are addicted to social media more than any other group. (Being a young, single female was most strongly associated with displaying addictive social media behavior. Addictive social media behavior was also

strongly related to narcissistic personality traits and low self-esteem.)

- The average smartphone user touches their device 2,617 times a day where heavy users can touch their device up to 5,427 times a day.
- Eighty percent of smartphone users check their phones within one hour before going to sleep, and 35 percent of whom do within five minutes.[94][95]

94 "These 8 Social Media Addiction Statistics Show Where We're Spending Our Time," *MedizKix*.

95 Arthur Zuckerman, "109 Technology Addiction Statistics 2020/2021 Data, Facts & Insights," *CompareCamp*, May 29, 2020.

Part III

So Gen-Z is pretty cool. But what does that mean, and what do we do now?

Chapter 14

Here's what you can do.

———

Are you Gen-Z?

Gen-Z is still young, but being young means being in power. Know your power and understand that there is no such thing as bad timing, and that you are capable of making change in the world. Use this as an inspiration for all the amazing things that our generation is doing, and what you could be doing. I'm sixteen as I'm writing this, and that's still pretty mind blowing to me.

I don't mean to sound corny, but the classic quote, "if there is a will, there is a way" is increasingly applicable in today's world. Everyone has their own circumstances, but for the most part, our generation has the world at our fingertips. We can look anything up at any time, connect to an esteemed professor about their research at a university, and listen in to some of the greatest minds on this planet with the click of a button.

We can do anything and everything. There are cons, but the pros outweigh them, and all you need to do is start. And yes, starting is the hard part. I'm a huge procrastinator, but starting is what makes us keep going.

Find your passions. I know, this is what every teacher, guidance counselor, or even parent tells you at some point in your life. But, finding your passion has never been easier. Attend virtual panels, virtual networking events, and reach out to people to talk to them about their occupation and see if you would be interested in them. Read up on current events, and if there's an even slightly interesting concept in school, go online and find the ten thousand other concepts that intersect with that particular one. In doing so, we are able to make connections, and move forward doing things that we love, versus signing ourselves up for a monotonous and uninteresting lifestyle that aims to serve others, and not ourselves.

The law of attraction states that if you like doing something and you are passionate about it, you will not only do that particular piece of work faster, but you will also do it more thoroughly and efficiently. And who knows? You might be on track to becoming the next Bill Gates. Finding our passions early on and working toward making career paths out of such passions will lead to our success because we will always be looking to move forward, and do the next big thing in that particular field. This is what will move our society forward; changemakers that are passionate about what they are doing and want to use their passions to improve the world.

Hey parents! This one's for you

Parents of Gen-Zers, you have the privilege of being able to see your child flourish and be a part of the largest and most diverse generation to date. You can work with them not only to promote intergenerational equity, but to learn from each other. Your child will most likely have something new to tell you about the world every single day. I know that my parents almost get annoyed with how many things I tell them over the course of a day, but in reality, I'm just learning about the world around me.

With that note, encourage the interests of your children, and allow for "screen time." Now, don't freak out on me.

I didn't say unrestricted screen time. You may deem certain sites should be blocked, which is your prerogative as a parent. I rather mean allow safe, general screen time because while devices like a computer and a phone can have games and distractions, they can also have ways for your children to become lifelong thinkers and learners.

I'll give you a relatively funny example. One of my friends and his mother couldn't get along because he spent "too much time on his phone." For his mom, she had no idea what he was doing, and she believed that he was wasting his time on his devices when there were several things that he needed to work on, like the SATs. What this mother didn't know was that her son was actually doing SAT prep online on his phone, and he ended up getting a perfect 1600 out of 1600 on the exam. The truth of the matter is that your son or daughter could be making the next Facebook. So, talk to your children, and help them embrace their potential!

Specific sites like Netflix or gaming sites can have screen time restrictions, but the internet might be helping more than hurting your kids.

However, parents, you do play a quintessential role in your child's development, and that is fostering the learning of soft skills. Soft skills are skills such as communication, working on a team, active listening, and openness. Such skills are important moving forward and might just be the difference between your child's application at a particular job, and the next person next to them. Soft skills are important in addition to all of the harder skills that Gen-Z can so easily acquire online, and parents can help facilitate learning them at home.

Companies—Yeah Mr. CEO, I'm talking to you.

Gen-Z is 2.4 billion people, representing 32 percent of the world's population and holding forty-four-billion-dollars-plus in buying power. Know Gen-Z before talking about them. Talk to Gen-Z about what matters to them before making assumptions, ads, marketing campaigns, and strategies. *You can't center strategy around a population that you don't know.* Gen-Z is innately in turn with what is going on in the world, and one day "lit" could be the cool fad word that we're using, but the next day we could be using something entirely different, like "guap."

We need to recognize that one size doesn't fit all when it comes to Gen-Z. What message are you trying to portray with your company and social media content that corresponds with any campaign, and ask yourself, who is this message resonating with? Is there a social good component to the campaign I'm putting out? What am I trying to portray to my audience? These questions are all valid, because Gen-Z values transparency and authenticity. We want to know, and we want to be part of a story with impact that you are creating as a company or a brand.

When Gen-Z enters the workforce

We come into the workforce with so much information, which is atypical of other generations as other generations had certain expectations, values, and almost traditions upon this entry. Gen-Z is different. We don't necessarily have these expectations or inhibitions because we have this already established knowledge about what to expect, whether that be reading it through a blog post or going on social media and researching.

So, we're not just social media freaks that can't live without our phones. We're invested in work culture and want to be posting about how cool our job is on our profiles. We're not just people who only speak in code, we actually care more about communication and understanding others' points of view. Talk to us, and not about us.

In addition to that, Gen-Z also has an idea of the issues that come up in a particular place of work, whether that be sexual assault, racial discrimination, or a gap in pay. But, with this knowledge comes this expectation that we're going to be the exception. For example, if I go into the workplace, I'm going to think that I'm going to be that one person who's not going to be sexually assaulted or I'm going to be that one person who's not going to suffer from the gender pay gap, but in reality, we aren't the exception but are rather a part of that statistic that we're trying to combat and prevent.

When it comes to Gen-Z, big brand marketing isn't the only way to reach the broad and diverse audience of Gen-Z. Macro, micro, and even nano influencers are the way to go in terms of creating genuine, authentic content for Gen-Z to resonate with. The particular brands that influencers decide to support need to be aligned to their previous content on their feed and resonate with the message or set of ideas that they put out. Gen-Z can identify that a random post in comparison to other meaningful ones on a creator's feed means that the product or company that they are promoting isn't an authentic relationship.

Every Gen-Zer online is trying to establish their own "personal brand" and brands and companies need to appeal to this. This can be achievable through more, but smaller, niche campaigns that can resonate with several different audiences and subgroups within the generation. This can even be supporting a different charity every month with a portion of sales supporting a particular organization, repackaging certain products in a more sustainable manner, or even having more inclusive packaging with neutral pronouns, steering away from stereotypical gender norms.

Gen-Z cares about the ethics and morality of a brand. A company's mission is the key to its success, and this mission needs to be apparent with every product and campaign. Gen-Z is more conscious as a generation and placing values at the core of a company shows Gen-Z that their money is being spent consciously and wisely in purchasing one's products.

The truth is self-evident: Gen-Z and their BS filter will be there, and they are not afraid to call you out. Make sure you're reaching out to Gen-Z to get a true reaction of what they think of a particular product, and how it should best be marketed, and with who specifically so that there is no question in terms of a lack of authenticity.

We like videos. TikTok, YouTube, vlogs, Snapchat, and more have led us to prefer this particular method of communication. So before spending half your budget on photos, maybe reach out to an influencer that could represent your brand and ask them to do a vlog using your products, and have them upload it to their social media accounts. This is more effective and will reach a broader audience. Utilizing community platforms and reading up on Reddit threads or spending some time on Depop or Pinterest might give you an idea of what Gen-Z is really thinking about, and possibly posting content on such platforms in a positive light as a solution to a particular problem may serve as an effective marketing strategy.

Short-form content is key. Our attention spans aren't very long. We're more likely to watch thirty one-minute videos compared to one long thirty-minute video. Keeping your content short and simple is absolutely necessary in grasping the attention of Gen-Z.

Our spending power is large, and we're willing to spend more to support issues that we care about; and support those that we care about. We're willing to be part of new trends, as long as that means not breaking the bank.

We also know that there is power in good technology. The power of Apple, for example, is widespread. Among Gen-Z, there is a somewhat collective hatred for Samsung and Android products although they may be superior, because having an iPhone, a Macintosh, or iPad is seen as better, and having Apple products can help Gen-Zers fit in. Even a "worse" model of an Apple device is better than having the best version of a Samsung device. So, if you're an app developer, maybe see if you can get your code on Apple's app store because you have a broader Gen-Z audience there.

Policymakers & legislators

Again, know Gen-Z. Also, know our world, because politically, we're not in a good place. With the internet, we are able to see what's going on across the country much easier and faster than before. We care about the state of our nation and want to be a part of a country that is acting on our interests and ideals, from the ground up. This is something that policymakers have to account for, and embrace in terms of campaign strategy, gaining votes, and proposing new policies.

Gen-Zers get the majority of their news from their social media feeds, and many of their feeds aren't as diverse as you might want them to be, with the algorithm tailoring content specifically for the particular individual. How are you changing your past methods and strategies to fit the new world of technology? Facebook ads are proving more effective than million-dollar TV ads, and you need people from Gen-Z to reach out to the new, vast generation of voters that might cost you an election if not reached out to.

The polarization in our world, and specifically in the United States, is frankly out of proportion, to put it nicely. There is always an extreme left, and an extreme right, and no middle. Gen-Z knows that this cannot continue into the future. Although some might say that Gen-Z is seemingly liberal, we are actually more conservative in terms of spending and our careers in the future, but strongly believe in equal rights for all, including minorities, women, and those in the LGBTQIA community.

Gen-Z wants to make change, and we want to support candidates that are as diverse in ethnicity and thought as we are. We want to push society forward, and we need you to make decisions that act with our best interests, and the interests of following generations, in mind.

Work to know your constituents, especially those that are in Gen-Z, because they can help you move forward and serve communities better than ever before.

Overall, Gen-Z bears an importance on essentially every person's life, whether it be CEO's next consumer base, to politician's next constituency. Either way, Gen-Z matters, and it is going to be making an impact on the world—and probably for the better.

Part IV

Peace out.
This is (hopefully)
what you learned

Chapter 15

My final words

———

So, give or take, there's about fifty thousand words in this book. If you've made it this far, congratulations on that milestone. I'm going to preface this conclusion by saying what I've learned through writing this book is that Gen-Z is only getting started. We hold immense power, and there is no predicting what is to come because we can do anything. I personally am just astonished by what my peers are doing as a Gen-Zer myself, and hope that this book can bring our world together, so that we can learn from, and about each other. So, with that, here are some lessons that you (hopefully) have learned from reading through this book.

1) Gen-Z is here to stay. We are the largest and most diverse generation to date. We understand that our world isn't black and white, and that diversity is a strength and not a weakness in our society. Gen-Z workplaces and spending are more diverse as well due to varied interests, and more emphasis on individuality.

2) We want change, and we want it now. We are equipped with the resources to change the world, so don't be surprised if the world looks and runs in a totally unexpected, beautiful

way twenty years from now. There is a collective desire to do better in our generation, stemming from all of the traumatic events that we have witnessed and have had to go through. This is another great power. Social good will be at the forefront of any successful business venture in the future.

3) We have the world at our fingertips. Everything is accessible to us. This can have its pros and cons; pros being that there is nothing that we can't do, and anything we want to learn about is there. The cons being that all of this information is overwhelming. Our current state of the world has made it so that we almost have no "off" switch, and this contributes to the mental health epidemic that plagues our generation, and the imposter syndrome that can develop because of it. This is our reality.

Take us seriously. In 2021, the world was rocked with how young investors, including Gen-Zers, shorted GameStop stock. I won't go into the whole phenomenon here, but we have the resources, and we can figure it out: fast. And if you want to get to know us, just ask.

4) We find community within our social networks. We are able to find similar traits and characteristics that can bond us to people that live in another country, thousands of miles away from us. You're a procrastinator? Me too. Join me on #procrastinator TikTok.

5) We're still human. We're also still young. We're still learning too. So, maybe cut us some slack, because we're here on this journey with you, and are essentially an unprecedented generation.

With all of that, what's stopping you from changing the world? It's not just Gen-Z that has such insights. As a society, we need to aim for intergenerational equity, where we can come together, move away from the polarization that exists within generations, and think about what we can each bring to the table. Gen-Z has the tech, Millennials hold us accountable with high expectations for society, where Gen-X has the lived experience, and the Baby Boomers have the soft skills. Using all of our fortes to find a happy medium that is beneficial for our society moving forward is what we need to do. So, what, Baby Boomers need to take a computer class? Your teacher at that computer class might need you to help them out with a situation at work. We are perfectly able and have the resources to make change; we just have to do it.

Okay yes, that's probably how every book ends, and I know it. But really, it's true. It's all about changing your mindset, wanting to make that change, and doing everything that you can to do so, truly.

So, you might be thinking, what about you, Riya? Throughout this book, I've written in a really conversational tone, because I felt like this was the best way to give it to all of you: the highs, the lows, and everything in between about Gen-Z. I will insert a quick but important caveat here. Like I stated in the Gen-Z dictionary, Gen-Z is moving at a thousand miles an hour sometimes. Something that might be popular or trendy one day could be cancelled the next. So, in twenty years? This book might be wrong. But this book is what I think, coupled with data, expert opinions, and a bit of my own experience as a Gen-Zer.

My goal with this book isn't to make money or become the next Oprah Winfrey (although I wouldn't mind it), but really, I hope that this book can be used as a tool for other generations to understand Gen-Z, and for Gen-Zers to understand ourselves a little better to promote intergenerational equity.

So, what have I taken from writing this book? Along with a lot of late nights writing and hours interviewing and putting together this book, I've realized what my generation is capable of. If you've made it this far, you can tell that this book is very tech positive overall and regards Gen-Z as change-makers and doers. And Gen-Z is all that. But there's also a lot that comes with the amazing things that my generation can do, such as mental health, addiction, and a serious reevaluation with our relationship between social media and ourselves needed in the future.

As of April 2021, when this book is published, I'm a senior in high school. Honestly, I can't wait to be talking about Gen-Z and putting this book out there.

Besides that? I'm living through a global pandemic, scrambling to write college applications, and trying to manage everything going on in my life.

But do I know I have the potential to make change? Yes. Do I know I have the capacity and resources to make that change? Yes. Do I know I'll be surrounded by changemakers wanting the same? Yes. So, my last thought is yes, change the world in whatever way you feel fit! But make it possible for you to do so. Look at some of the big ideas in this book, grow your network, expand on your interests, and never limit yourself, because you can do it. You have the power, and you CAN change the world.

I admit there's a bit of preaching before I've practiced there, but I'll be with you all on this journey to understand Gen-Z better, and to be a part of the global revolution, in every sense, that we'll be leading.

Acknowledgements

I'd like acknowledge those who have given this book legs strong enough to move forward:

Kristin Osika, Madeline Fidellow, William Diep, Dhiraj Chhabra, Joe Krakoviak, Jasmine Lucas, Melissa Kilby, Lisa Touzeau, Kimberlee Rose, Harish Kambhampati, Carmen Gordillo, Lindsay Stein, Hallie Meyer, Marissa Blodnik, Clara Scholl, Eric Koester, Carol Cropp, Ken Fong, Komal Abhichandani, Anjali Arya, Caritas Ng, Deepa Krishna, Kuan Yin Knoll, Shubha Pandit, Reema Hussain, Raj Maan, Emma Svetvilas, Jaspreet Kaur, Anant Gupta, Anna Blue, Anastasia Leahy, Jivahn Moradian, Christopher Reilly, Nancy Reilly, Sarah Reilly, Anne Canter, Ava McDonald, Pamela Romanchuk, Jason-Lamont Jackson Sr., Michelle Schultz, Debra Coen, Girl Up, Srividya Ramamurthy, Bindu Khanna, Suhail Khan, Sushmita Srivastav, Maria Blanco, Michael Denburg, Kimya Jackson, Sierra RyanWallick, Robert Parisi, Gary Silverstrom, Tim Rehm, Aditya Desai, Vijay Jajoo, Alexander Purcell, Sangeeta Badlani, Bert Maes, Tony Edelstein, Zoe Jenkins, Maxwell Polsky, Sahiti Tholeti, David Cubie, Grace Goodwin, and Jasmine Tong.

I'd also like to acknowledge my mother. Thank you for always believing in me, having my back through whatever venture I pick up next, and always having time to talk no matter how busy you are. I love you.

Lastly, I'd like to acknowledge all of my interviewees in this book:

Connor Blakely, Ziad Ahmed, Sophia Delrosario, Madeline Allison, Nadya Okamoto, Dylan Miars, Lesley Jane Seymour, Jasmine Cheng, Melissa Kilby, Anna Blue, Neal Sivadas, Kristina Ang, Hallie Meyer, Matt Sarafa, Katie Tracy, Lucie Zhang, Maria Bobila, and Lindsay Stein.

Appendix

———

Introduction

Dimock, Michael. "Defining generations: Where Millennials end and Generation Z begins." *Pew Research Center,* January 17, 2019. https://www.pewresearch.org/fact-tank/2019/01/17/where-Millennials-end-and-generation-z-begins/.

Fontein, Dara. "Everything Social Marketers Need to Know About Generation Z." *Hootsuite,* November 13, 2019. https://blog.hootsuite.com/generation-z-statistics-social-marketers/#:~:-text=Market%20research%20shows%20that%2085,with%20brands%20on%20social%2C%20too.&text=Before%20makin-g%20a%20purchase%2C%20Gen,Millennials%20to%20turn%20to%20YouTube.

The History and Science of Change

Blakemore, Erin. "Youth in Revolt: Five Powerful Movements Fueled by Young Activists." *National Geographic,* March 23, 2018. https://www.nationalgeographic.com/culture/article/youth-activism-young-protesters-historic-movements.

Brueck, Hilary. "Greta Thunberg at UN Youth Climate Summit: 'We young people are unstoppable." *Insider News,* September 21, 2019. https://www.insider.com/greta-thunberg-un-youth-climate-summit-young-people-are-unstoppable-2019-9.

Divecha, Diana. "How Teens Today Are Different from Past Generations." *Greater Good Magazine,* October 20, 2017. https://greatergood.berkeley.edu/article/item/how_teens_today_are_different_from_past_generations#:~:text=iGens%20exhibit%20more%20care%20for%20others.&text=Yet%20as%20a%20result%2C%20they,may%20be%20distressing%20to%20some.

"Greta Thunberg tells world leaders 'you are failing us', as nations announce fresh climate action." *United Nations Department of Economic and Social Affairs.* September 24, 2019. https://www.un.org/development/desa/youth/news/2019/09/greta-thunberg/.

"Greta Thunberg quotes: 10 famous lines from teen activist." *BBC News,* September 25, 2019. https://www.bbc.co.uk/newsround/49812183.

"Is Your Business Ready for the Rise of Generation Z?" *Digital Marketing Institute,* October 14, 2016. https://digitalmarketinginstitute.com/blog/is-your-business-ready-for-the-rise-of-generation-z.

Lawford, Heather. *The Role of Attachment and Caregiving in the Emergence of Generativity from Early to Middle Adolescence.* (Concordia University, June 2008).

https://spectrum.library.concordia.ca/976134/1/NR42545.pdf.

Stein, Joel. "Millennials: The Me Me Me Generation- Why Millennials will save us all." *Time Magazine,* May 20, 2013. http://content.time.com/time/subscriber/article/0,33009,2143001,00.html.

"What is intersectionality, and what does it have to do with me?." *YW Boston* , March 29, 2017. https://www.ywboston.org/2017/03/what-is-intersectionality-and-what-does-it-have-to-do-with-me/.

Ziad Ahmed speaking at *Digital Marketing Expo and Conference,* September 7- 8, 2021. ziadahmed.me.

Why Now?

Abby Gillmer (@abby_gillmer). "You're teaching us how to hate the thing we want to love the most-students." TikTok video, June 26, 2020.

JUV Consulting. "Memes and Movements: 20 Trends that defined Gen Z in 2020." *JUV Consulting,* January 19, 2020. https://www.juv2020.com/.

Oxford Languages, Lexico. s.v. "futurism (n.)" Accessed Feb 26 2021. https://www.lexico.com/en/definition/futurism.

Poague, Emily. "Gen Z Is Shaping a New Era of Learning: Here's What you Should Know." *LinkedIn Learning Blog,* December 18, 2018. https://www.linkedin.com/business/learning/blog/learning-and-development/gen-z-is-shaping-a-new-era-of-learning-heres-what-you-should-kn.

Tech, tech, and more tech

Charli D'amelio (@charlidamelio) account on TikTok. Accessed February 27, 2021.

Dixie D'amelio (@dixiedamelio) account on TikTok. Accessed February 27, 2021.

Hebblethwaite, Colm. "Gen Z engaging with 10 hours of online content a day." *Marketing Tech,* February 9th, 2018. https://marketingtechnews.net/news/2018/feb/09/gen-z-engaging-10-hours-online-content-day/.

JUV Consulting. "Memes and Movements: 20 Trends that defined Gen Z in 2020." *JUV Consulting,* January 19, 2020. https://www.juv2020.com/.

Okamoto, Nadya. "Generation Z: A Generation Of Distrust And Disruption." *Advertising Week 360,* September 10, 2019. https://www.advertisingweek360.com/what-generation-z-think-of-generation-z/.

Opfer, Chris. "Our Online Personalities Change Across Different Social Media Platforms." *How Stuff Works,* May 27, 2017. https://computer.howstuffworks.com/internet/social-networking/networks/online-personality-change-social-media.htm#:~:text=Our%20Online%20Personalities%20Change%20Across%20Different%20Social%20Media%20Platforms,-by%20Chris%20Opfer&text=In%20fact%2C%20a%20new%20study,just%20want%20to%20fit%20in.

Taylor, Kate. "Gen Z is more conservative than many realize — but the Instagram-fluent generation will revolutionize the right." *Business Insider, The State of Gen-Z.* https://www.businessinsider.com/gen-z-changes-political-divides-2019-7.

yup… tech has its downsides

Bernazzani, Sophia. "7 Soft Skills You Need to Achieve Career Growth." *HubSpot Blog,* November 16, 2017. https://blog.hubspot.com/marketing/soft-skills.

Bromwich, Jonah Engel. "Everyone is Canceled." *The New York Times,* June 28, 2018. https://www.nytimes.com/2018/06/28/style/is-it-canceled.html.

Centers for Disease Control and Prevention. "Sleep in Middle and High School Students." accessed February 26, 2021, https://www.cdc.gov/healthyschools/features/students-sleep.htm#:~:-text=How%20much%20sleep%20someone%20needs,10%20hours%20per%2024%20hours.

Heid, Markham. "Depression and Suicide Rates Are Rising Sharply in Young Americans, New Report Says. This May Be One Reason Why." *Time,* March 14, 2019. https://time.com/5550803/depression-suicide-rates-youth/.

Merriam-Webster. s.v. "canceled" Accessed Feb 26 2021. https://www.merriam-webster.com/words-at-play/cancel-culture-words-were-watching#:~:text=To%20cancel%20someone%20(usually%20a,or%20promoting%20a%20writer's%20works.

Popken, Ben. "Did Video Games and iPads Kill Toys R Us?" *NBC News,* September 19, 2017. https://www.nbcnews.com/business/consumer/did-video-games-ipads-kill-toys-r-us-n802751.

"The Psychology of Being 'Liked' on Social Media." *Start Digital,* November 27, 2017. https://medium.com/swlh/likes-on-social-media-87bfff679602.

The Social Dilemma, Netflix. Directed by Jeff Orlowski, screenplay by Jeff Orlowski, Vickie Curtis, and Davis Coombe, produced by Larissa Rhodes and Exposure Labs. https://www.netflix.com/search?q=the%20social&jbv=81254224.

"What are cookies?" *Norton LifeLock,* August 12, 2019. https://us.norton.com/internetsecurity-privacy-what-are-cookies.html.

Access to resources
Law, Thomas J. "10 Vital Strategies to use When Marketing to Gen-Z." *Oberlo,* November 3, 2020. https://www.oberlo.com/blog/marketing-strategies-generation-z.

Taylor, Kate. "Instagram is Gen Z's go-to source of political news — and it's already having an impact on the 2020 election." *Business Insider,* July 1, 2019. https://www.businessinsider.com/gen-z-gets-its-political-news-from-instagram-accounts-2019-6.

Talentless? More like Talent filled
Curtin, Denise. "James Charles' Morphe palette sells out in less than 10 minutes after going on sale." *Her.* November 13, 2018. https://www.her.ie/beauty/james-charles-morphe-palette-sells-less-10-minutes-going-sale-435917.

Fashion. Statista. https://www.statista.com/outlook/244/100/fashion/worldwide.

Hurtado, Cayatena. "The Subtle Art of (Not) Understanding Gen Z." *Product Hunt.* https://www.producthunt.com/stories/the-subtle-art-of-not-understanding-gen-z.

Smith, Lilly. "The clothing of the future completely dissolves after use." *Fast Company,* August 31, 2020. https://www.fastcompany.com/90544924/the-clothing-of-the-future-completely-dissolves-after-use#:~:text=Scarlett%20Yang%2C%20a%20recent%20graduate,The%20textile%20is%20completely%20biodegradable.

Stanton, Audrey. "What Is Fast Fashion, Anyway?" *The Good Trade.* October 8, 2018. https://www.thegoodtrade.com/features/what-is-fast-fashion.

Decisions, and performative ones too

"How Consumer Segmentation Helps Your Marketing Goals." *CMG Consulting,* November 10, 2020. https://www.cmgconsulting.com/post/what-is-consumersegmentation.

McDowell, Jason. "Is Generation Z Too Interdependent – or Is That the Future of Work?" *Recruiter.com* November 21, 2016.

https://www.recruiter.com/i/is-generation-z-too-interdependent-or-is-that-the-future-of-work/.

Talk to us, not about us

Jasper, Lisa. "Reverse mentoring: 5 key reasons your business needs it." *Insperity.* https://www.insperity.com/blog/reverse-mentoring/.

The Gen-Z Dictionary

Benberry, Imani. "Dear Non-Black People, AAVE Is Not 'Stan' Or 'Internet Culture." *Study Breaks,* August 24, 2020. https://studybreaks.com/thoughts/aave-not-stan-culture/.

Berhe, Meron. "AAVE isn't Gen Z slang." *The Pitch, Walter Johnson High School Student Newspaper.* January 4, 2021. https://www.wjpitch.com/opinion/2021/01/14/aave-isnt-gen-z-slang/.

Blay, Zeba. "12 Words Black People Invented, And White People Killed." *The Huffington Post.* August 20, 2015. https://www.huffpost.com/entry/black-slang-white-people-ruined_n_55c-cda07e4b064d5910ac8b3.

Brennan, William. "Julie Washington's Quest to Get Schools to Respect African-American English." *The Atlantic.* April 15, 2018. https://www.theatlantic.com/magazine/archive/2018/04/the-code-switcher/554099/.

@brendanrouthRETURNS Reddit page. Accessed February 16, 2020. https://www.reddit.com/r/rpdrcringe/comments/k0154b/trixie_calls_for_aave_to_be_cancelled_in_2021/.

Cardoza, Nicole. "Respect AAVE." *Anti-Racism Daily.* July 16, 2020. https://www.antiracismdaily.com/archives/respect-aave-anti-racism-daily.

Coghill, Arianna. "The Truth Behind Ebonics." *HerCampus,* January 27, 2017. https://www.hercampus.com/school/vcu/truth-behind-ebonics.

Jackson Michele, Lauren. "We Need to Talk About Digital Blackface in Reaction GIFs." *Teen Vogue*. August 2, 2017. https://www.teenvogue.com/story/digital-blackface-reaction-gifs.

Jones, Taylor. "What is AAVE?." *Language Jones*. September 19, 2014. https://www.languagejones.com/blog-1/2014/6/8/what-is-aave.

@kllingf (Iliana) Twitter Page. Accessed February 16, 2020. https://twitter.com/kllinggf/status/1345579374196764672.

Oxford Languages. s.v. "echo chamber (n.)" Accessed Feb 26 2021. https://www.oxfordlearnersdictionaries.com/us/definition/english/echo-chamber#:~:text=echo%20chamber-,-noun,not%20have%20to%20consider%20alternatives.

Tremeer, Eleanor. "Is It Cultural Appropriation To Use Drag Slang And AAVE?." *Babbel Magazine*. January 8, 2019. https://www.babbel.com/en/magazine/cultural-appropriation-drag-slang-aave.

Urban Dictionary, s.v. "skinny legend (a.)," accessed February 25, 2021, https://www.urbandictionary.com/define.php?term=skinny%20legend.

Urban Dictionary, s.v. "cottagecore (a.)," accessed February 25, 2021 https://www.urbandictionary.com/define.php?term=cottage%20core.

Zenerations Instagram page, post about AAVE. Accessed February 10, 2020. https://www.instagram.com/p/CLIBhJajkrJ/.

Zenerations Instagram page, post about Black cultural fashion trends. Accessed February 10, 2020. https://www.instagram.com/p/CLIBhJajkrJ/.

Desire to be better—what does that mean and why is that important to us?

American Psychological Association. "Stress in America, Generation Z." October 2018. https://www.apa.org/news/press/releases/stress/2018/stress-gen-z.pdf.

Beattie, Andrew. "How to Calculate the Return on Investment (ROI) of a Marketing Campaign." Updated March 2, 2020. https://www.investopedia.com/articles/personal-finance/053015/how-calculate-roi-marketing-campaign.asp.

"Burnout Prevention and Treatment." *HelpGuide.* October 2020. https://www.helpguide.org/articles/stress/burnout-prevention-and-recovery.htm#:~:text=Burnout%20reduces%20productivity%20and%20saps,%2C%20work%2C%20and%20social%20life.

Hawkins, Erica. "Importance of ROI: Why it matters for all businesses." *Call Rail.* https://www.callrail.com/blog/importance-of-roi-why-it-matters-for-all-businesses/.

United States Department of Agriculture Economic Research Service. "Access to Affordable and Nutritious Food: Measuring and Understanding Food Deserts and Their Consequences." United States Department of Agriculture, 2009. Web Accessed February 21, 2021. https://www.dosomething.org/us/facts/11-facts-about-food-deserts.

"Why Do Different Generation Use Social Media?." *Marketing Charts,* October 21, 2019. https://www.marketingcharts.com/digital/social-media-110652.

Wust, MaryKate."How Gen Z Can Swap Burnout for Breakthroughs." *Penn Medicine News,* March 21, 2019. https://www.pennmedicine.org/news/news-blog/2019/march/how-gen-z-can-swap-burnout-for-breakthroughs.

Collective trauma, and bridging generations
Merriam Webster Dictionary, s.v. "trauma (*n.*)." Accessed February 2, 2021.

"These 8 Social Media Addiction Statistics Show Where We're Spending Our Time." *MedizKix.* https://mediakix.com/blog/social-media-addiction-statistics/.

Zuckerman, Arthur. "109 Technology Addiction Statistics 2020/2021 Data, Facts & Insights." *CompareCamp.* May 29, 2020. https://comparecamp.com/technology-addiction-statistics/.